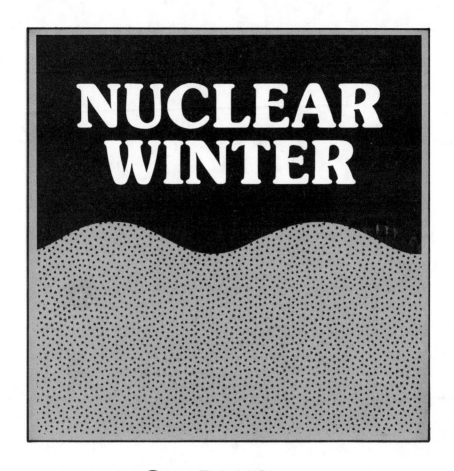

NUCLEAR WINTER

Gary E. McCuen

IDEAS IN CONFLICT SERIES

publications inc.

411 Mallalieu Drive
Hudson, Wisconsin 54016

Illustration & photo credits
Chuck Asay 72, 85, Ollie Harrington 41, 104, House Committee on Science and Technology 48, *Imprimis* 97, Charles Keller 120, Craig MacIntosh 113, Physicians for Social Responsibility 20, Sack 91, David Seavey 47, Carol & Simpson 79, Stayskal 39, U.S. Air Force 28, U.S. Congress 127, U.S. Dept. of Defense 28, War Resisters League 13, World Federalist Association 62.

© 1987 by Gary E. McCuen Publications, Inc.
411 Mallalieu Drive • Hudson, Wisconsin 54016
(715) 386-5662
International Standard Book Number 0-86596-062-3
Printed in the United States of America

CONTENTS

Ideas in Conflict   6

CHAPTER 1   INTRODUCTION

SUMMARY   9

1   BACKGROUND AND PERSPECTIVES ON THE
    ENVIRONMENTAL AND CLIMATIC EFFECTS
    OF NUCLEAR WAR   10

2   EXPERTS DEBATE THEORY OF NUCLEAR
    WINTER   17

3   NUCLEAR WINTER AND STRATEGIC POLICY   25

CHAPTER 2   NUCLEAR WINTER:
                IDEAS IN CONFLICT

4   DESTROYING GLOBAL CIVILIZATION   34
    *Carl Sagan and Physicians for
    Social Responsibility*
5   NUCLEAR WINTER IS IMPROBABLE   43
    Edward Teller
6   REPORTS ARE GREATLY EXAGGERATED   51
    George Rathjens
7   BIOLOGICAL EFFECTS OF NUCLEAR WINTER   57
    Stephen J. Gould

CHAPTER 3   NUCLEAR STRATEGY AND
                NUCLEAR WINTER

8   NO NEED TO CHANGE U.S. NUCLEAR
    STRATEGY   67
    Caspar Weinberger
9   STRATEGY CHANGES ARE MANDATORY   74
    Anthony E. Scoville

10 LIMITED NUCLEAR WAR STRATEGY MAY BE
    NECESSARY   81
    Leon Sloss
11 PLANNING NUCLEAR WAR-FIGHTING
    STRATEGIES IS INSANE   87
    Physicians for Social Responsibility
12 STRATEGIC DEFENSE AND NUCLEAR WINTER:
    THE POINT   93
    Richard Perle
13 STRATEGIC DEFENSE AND NUCLEAR WINTER:
    THE COUNTERPOINT   99
    Theodore A. Postol

**CHAPTER 4   PREVENTING A NUCLEAR
                    HOLOCAUST**

14 A NUCLEAR WAR IS IMPROBABLE   109
    Fred Schwarz
15 WE ARE CLOSE TO EXTINCTION   115
    Union of Concerned Scientists
16 CIVIL DEFENSE AND SURVIVAL: THE POINT   122
    Leon Goure
17 CIVIL DEFENSE AND SURVIVAL: THE
    COUNTERPOINT   129
    Leon Baya

Bibliography: Selected Literature Reviewed   136

Glossary of Terms   139

Abbreviations   140

REASONING SKILL DEVELOPMENT

These activities may be used as individualized study guides
for students in libraries and resource centers or as discussion catalysts in small group and classroom discussions.

1   Examining Counterpoints   31
2   Recognizing Author's Point of View   64
3   Interpreting Editorial Cartoons   106
4   What is Political Bias?   133

This series features ideas in conflict on political, social and moral issues. It presents counterpoints, debates, opinions, commentary and analysis for use in libraries and classrooms. Each title in the series uses one or more of the following basic elements:

Introductions that present an issue overview giving historic background and/or a description of the controversy.

Counterpoints and debates carefully chosen from publications, books, and position papers on the political right and left to help librarians and teachers respond to requests that treatment of public issues be fair and balanced.

Symposiums and forums that go beyond debates that can polarize and oversimplify. These present commentary from across the political spectrum that reflect how complex issues attract many shades of opinion.

A global emphasis with foreign perspectives and surveys on various moral questions and political issues that will help readers to place subject matter in a less culture-bound and ethno-centric frame of reference. In an ever shrinking and interdependent world, understanding and cooperation are essential. Many issues are global in nature and can be effectively dealt with only by common efforts and international understanding.

Reasoning skill study guides and discussion activities provide ready made tools for helping with critical reading and evaluation of content. The guides and activities deal with one or more of the following:

RECOGNIZING AUTHOR'S POINT OF VIEW

INTERPRETING EDITORIAL CARTOONS

VALUES IN CONFLICT

WHAT IS EDITORIAL BIAS?

WHAT IS SEX BIAS?
WHAT IS POLITICAL BIAS?
WHAT IS ETHNOCENTRIC BIAS?
WHAT IS RACE BIAS?
WHAT IS RELIGIOUS BIAS?

*From across **the political spectrum** varied sources are presented for research projects and classroom discussions. Diverse opinions in the series come from magazines, newspapers, syndicated columnists, books, political speeches, foreign nations, and position papers by corporations and non-profit institutions.*

About the Editor

Gary E. McCuen is an editor and publisher of anthologies for public libraries and curriculum materials for schools. Over the past 16 years his publications of over 200 titles have specialized in social, moral and political conflict. They include books, pamphlets, cassettes, tabloids, filmstrips and simulation games, many of them designed from his curriculums during 11 years of teaching junior and senior high school social studies. At present he is the editor and publisher of the *Ideas in Conflict* series and the *Editorial Forum* series.

CHAPTER 1

INTRODUCTION

SUMMARY

1 BACKGROUND AND PERSPECTIVES ON
THE ENVIRONMENTAL AND CLIMATIC
EFFECTS OF NUCLEAR WAR

2 EXPERTS DEBATE THEORY OF
NUCLEAR WINTER

3 NUCLEAR WINTER AND STRATEGIC
POLICY

Summary

This chapter examines scientific and policy implications of nuclear winter. It is based on extensive review of relevant literature and detailed discussions with a wide range of scientists, researchers, and policy analysts within and outside of government. It provides an overview of what is known about nuclear winter and of ongoing research addressing areas of scientific uncertainty. It also outlines potential implications for defense strategy, arms control, and foreign policy-making and points out the absence of a consensus on the need for policy changes at this time.

"Nuclear winter"—a term used to describe potential long-term climatic and environmental effects of nuclear war—has been the subject of recent controversy. Scientists are researching the possibility that surface temperatures could be dramatically reduced by large quantities of sun-blocking smoke and dust particles injected high into the atmosphere, which could affect the survivors of a nuclear war. According to the theory, distant countries not directly involved could also be affected.

The controversy surrounding nuclear winter has polarized views about its scientific basis and potential policy implications. This chapter provides (1) an overview of the science of nuclear winter, (2) pertinent information for considering policy implications, and (3) the status of U.S. research.

INTRODUCTION

BACKGROUND AND PERSPECTIVES ON THE ENVIRONMENTAL AND CLIMATIC EFFECTS OF NUCLEAR WAR

Until recently, scientific research had not comprehensively addressed the potential long-term climatic and environmental damage of a nuclear conflict. History contains examples of fire induced smoke clouds such as from World War II bombings, including the limited nuclear war on Japan, and large scale fires of more recent origin. Due to the limited nature of these occurrences and the lack of previous appreciation for the potential effects, there is incomplete recorded measurement data from those events applicable to assessing and predicting environmental consequences. Now, however, scientific research suggests that a nuclear conflict could inject enough smoke and dust particles into the atmosphere to block out sunlight and cause severe drops in surface temperatures over a significant period of time. This, in turn, could adversely affect plants, animals, and humans.

Excerpted from a report by the U.S. Government Accounting Office titled *Nuclear Winter's Uncertainties Surround the Long-Term Effects of Nuclear War,* March, 1986, pp. 8-14.

The term "nuclear winter" has been coined to describe these effects. The implications of the theory are global in nature; preliminary research suggests that noninvolved nations, as well as those directly involved, could be vulnerable to the climatic and environmental effects.

The nuclear winter issue has sparked much congressional interest not only in the science associated with the theory but also in its relevent national security implications. The Congress has legislatively mandated administration reports on the subject. Also, the administration has funded some nuclear winter research since fiscal year 1983 and has recently begun an interagency research program chaired by the President's Office of Science and Technology Policy (OSTP). To date, because of the preliminary nature of scientific research, the administration has not acknowledged any ramifications of the nuclear winter theory that would change defense policy or programs. Although varying views exist, there is no consensus for action at this time.

Climatic Effects

In 1975, the National Academy of Sciences issued a report, "Long-Term Worldwide Effects of Multiple Nuclear-Weapons Detonations," which estimated the global radioactive fallout, ozone depletion and climatic effects from a nuclear exchange and the resulting effect on ecosystems, aquatic life, and people. The climatic effects were theorized to arise from dust placed in the stratosphere by near-surface nuclear blasts. These effects were concluded to be relatively small compared to current estimates. As the first attempt to quantify all the known or conjectured long-term effects of nuclear war, the report concluded that the most significant and the only potentially long-term catastrophic global scale effects were those resulting from the ozone depletion, which would allow more unfiltered ultraviolet rays to reach the earth's surface. Debate continues today on the importance of ozone depletion, and many uncertainties still exist as to the potential effects of radioactive fallout.

In 1979, the Office of Technology Assessment issued a report, "The Effects of Nuclear War," which focused mainly on the immediate consequences. The long-term effects discussed in the report centered on those generated from exposure to high levels of radioactive fallout, namely, cancer

11

and genetic diseases. The report did note, however, that a large nuclear war could possibly produce irreversible adverse effects on the environment and ecological system. Since many scientific processes involved were still not well understood, the report stated that it was not possible to estimate the probability or the probable magnitude of such damage.

In the 1980's some scientists introduced a new variable into the study of nuclear war effects—smoke and its long-term climatic and environmental damage which goes beyond any previously recognized dimensions.

Long Term Effects

In 1980, AMBIO, the environmental journal of the Royal Swedish Academy of Sciences, commissioned a series of studies on nuclear war. One such study published in June 1982, "The Atmosphere After a Nuclear War: Twilight at Noon," attempted to quantify for the first time the possible impact of smoke from burning forests and cities. According to its authors, Paul Crutzen of the Max Plank Institute for Chemistry in West Germany and John Birks from the University of Colorado, fires pushing smoke into the atmosphere could cause serious long-term effects. Crutzen and Birks speculated that the amount of smoke likely to be generated by such fires would be sufficient to reduce the incoming solar energy at the earth's surface for periods of several weeks or longer. They conjectured that smoke combined with dust raised from near-surface explosions would form a dark cloud at least over large areas of the northern hemisphere[1] and reduce the influx of light below the level required for photosynthesis. This study by Crutzen and Birks brought new attention to the potential long-term effects of nuclear war.

TTAPS Study

Public awareness of the nuclear winter issue came most prominently from the highly publicized work of five scien-

---

[1]Nuclear winter studies are generally predicated on a nuclear conflict occurring in the northern hemisphere.

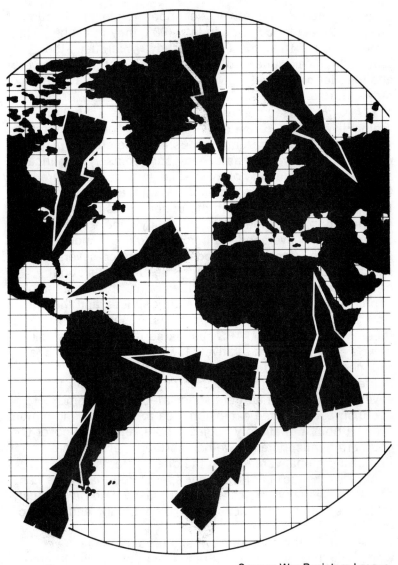

tists who, in conjunction with their own analysis and modeling efforts, were able to build on the findings of Crutzen and

Birks and more quantitatively describe the global climatic effect of a nuclear conflict. In late 1983, they published what is now referred to as the TTAPS[2] study, which used the phrase "nuclear winter" to describe the hypothesized severe and long-term effects involving continental-scale subfreezing temperatures.

TTAPS addressed numerous global effects, including radioactive fallout, ozone depletion, and production of toxic chemicals and gases from combustion. The study's major contribution, however, has been described as systematically analyzing the sequence of events; i.e., war scenario, fire ignition, smoke production, atmospheric injection, and finally the absorption of sunlight in the upper atmosphere and the resultant cooling of the earth. The study used a computer-driven, globally averaged mathematical climate model to postulate the effects. This model incorporated several war scenarios and contained numerous assumptions about critical variables, such as how cities burn, how much smoke is produced, where it goes in the atmosphere, and the optical properties of the smoke particles. Based on one of these war scenarios, TTAPS calculated that nuclear smoke clouds generated by a relatively low level of explosions (e.g., 100 megatons) could cool the earth's surface by 36° to 72° Fahrenheit and that temperatures might not recover for several months. The authors speculated that the smoke could spread from the explosion area to the attacking nation, even without a retaliatory nuclear strike, and could cover the southern hemisphere (as well as northern), even if that portion of the globe were spared the direct effects of the nuclear exchange. TTAPS further speculated that human and other species survivors of a nuclear blast would be seriously threatened by long-term exposure to cold, dark, and radioactivity.

These dramatic and controversial predictions received world-wide media attention. Some scientists, including those in the Department of Defense (DOD), stated that the effects

[2]TTAPS is derived from the authors' last names: R. Turco from R&D Associates; O.Toon, T. Ackerman, and J. Pollack from NASA AMES; and C. Sagan from Cornel University. TTAPS author Richard Turco is recognized as having coined the term nuclear winter.

of smoke from a nuclear explosion had gone virtually un-
noticed within the scientific community. Others were critical
of the TTAPS predictions, calling them premature because of
the limitations they found in the assumptions and computer
climate model used in the study.

National Academy Study

One of the more authoritative assessments of the possible
atmospheric effects of nuclear war was published in
December 1984 by the National Academy of Sciences (NAS).
Requested and funded by DOD in early 1983, the NAS
assessment essentially echoed the preliminary TTAPS
results and stated that long-term climatic effects with severe
implications were plausible. Based on the study assumptions, which included a 6,500 megaton nuclear conflict, the
report showed that during the summer months land surface
temperatures could be reduced from 50° to 77° Fahrenheit in
the northern hemisphere for a period of several weeks.
Serious biological and agricultural problems could result due
to the abrupt and long lasting atmospheric change. The NAS
report also speculated that nations far removed from the
target areas, including the attacking nation, could be
vulnerable.

NAS scientists stated that because of uncertainties in the
assumptions used, as well as limitations in computer
climate models, they could not subscribe with confidence to
any specific quantitative conclusions drawn from their
calculations. Essentially, they believed that the estimates of
the potential consequences have utility only as an indicator
of the seriousness of what might occur. NAS nevertheless
stressed that the potential long-term consequences of a major nuclear exchange had worldwide implications which
should be included in any analysis of the consequences of
nuclear war. NAS also believed that a major effort to narrow
the scientific uncertainties was needed. . . .

International Community

The international scientific community is also studying the
nuclear winter issue. The Royal Society of Canada published
a Canadian appraisal of nuclear winter and its associated ef-

fects in January 1985.[3] The report, based on the analysis of numerous consultants mainly from the United States and Canada, concluded that nuclear winter is a credible and formidable threat which could last for several months and cause severe damage or destruction to crops and vegetation. It recommended that the Canadian government immediately consider the military, strategic, and social consequences of such a major climatic effect, notwithstanding the many scientific uncertainties in the theory.

Scientists from other countries, such as Australia and West Germany, continue to conduct research into the nuclear winter theory. In addition, a committee (Scientific Committee on Problems of the Environment—SCOPE) of the International Council of Scientific Unions, in September 1985, completed a 3-year study focusing on nuclear winter. Scientists from numerous countries, including the United States and U.S.S.R., worked on the study. They researched the physical and atmospheric consequences of nuclear war as well as the biological, agricultural, and human implications. SCOPE concluded that indirect effects (the latter implications) of a large scale nuclear war could be potentially more consequential globally than the direct effects. The report recommended continued research on the entire range of implications with close interaction between biologists and physical scientists.

[3]"Nuclear Winter and Associated Effects: A Canadian Appraisal of the Environmental Impact of Nuclear War," The Royal Society of Canada, January 31, 1985.

INTRODUCTION

EXPERTS DEBATE THEORY
OF NUCLEAR WINTER

The term nuclear winter has recently gained common usage, yet some have viewed it to be an unfortunate label in that current scientific research cannot definitively confirm or refute the extreme effects predicted by the theory. The most common point of agreement is the new recognition that a nuclear war is apt to result in adverse climatic, environmental, or biological impact, but of uncertain scale and duration. Scientists in DOD, government laboratories, and private and university research centers all recognize that significant uncertainties and unknowns exist with the theory. Despite differing views, they agree that these uncertainties need to be studied.

Nuclear winter uncertainties can be placed in three categories: war scenarios, fire and atmospheric research, and computer atmospheric modeling. While some of the uncertainties cannot be resolved or known absent a nuclear conflict, knowledge of others can be refined and the unknowns of some others, at best, can only be deduced. Some scientists believe it may be 5 years or longer before the uncertainties will be reduced to the point where more widely accepted projections could be made on the climatic and environmental consequences of nuclear war. Other scientists believe significant incremental increases in knowledge could occur over shorter timeframes.

Excerpted from a report by the U.S. Government Accounting Office titled *Nuclear Winter's Uncertainties Surround the Long-Term Effects of Nuclear War,* March, 1986, pp. 16-24.

War Scenario Variables can only be Assumed

Highly classified plans provide the details for waging a nuclear war, but the actual course of events and the prevailing conditions are impossible to know in advance.

Given the highly classified nature of war plans, scientists must base their research to some extent on speculation or unclassified informed opinion about the likely targets of nuclear weapons. They cannot know in advance, for example, the number and yield of weapons which would actually be used, the distributions of targets against which those weapons would be directed, or the number of weapons which would actually reach their targets and detonate successfully. In addition, an adversary's response during a nuclear conflict will not be known in advance.

Another variable is whether the bombs will explode in the air or upon impact. This is an important variable since each type of blast would inject different quantities of dust into the atmosphere and block out the sun to varying degrees. NAS scientists note that the climatic and environmental effects depicted in their 1984 report could be several times larger if a combatant decided to rely more on groundbursts in a war because they would likely inject the most dust into the atmosphere. Fire and resulting smoke and soot generation are also affected by altitude of detonation, but to a much smaller degree than dust.

The time (season) of the year also matters greatly, according to nuclear winter theory. A smoke cloud from a nuclear exchange in July could severely affect crops and plant life if the resulting temperature decease is significant. Yet, the same exchange in January could have little or no effect in the northern hemisphere, depending on its duration and spread, if it occurs where temperatures are normally cold at that time of year. Finally, weather conditions existing in a target area could mitigate long-term effects. For example, moisture tends to "wash-out" smoke and dust particles before they can get very high into the atmosphere.

Given the intrinsically uncertain nature of these variables, scientists must make critical assumptions for their nuclear winter simulations and cannot therefore offer definitive predictions. Some scientists claim that a small number of high yield weapons, specifically targeted, can produce severe climatic and environmental results. This claim has fostered an apparent misconception that going beyond a specific "threshold" would trigger a nuclear winter. Scientific research cannot now prove this with any accuracy. Most scientists note that too many independent variables (e.g., combustible target, groundburst, clear weather, etc.) would have to occur in a precise fashion before a small number of nuclear weapons could create long-term climatic and environmental effects. They indicate that if a threshold does exist it is more likely to be in terms of the amount of smoke, soot, and dust particles injected into the atmosphere rather than in the number of weapons or the megatonnage used.

Fire Research is Crucial in Determining Nuclear Winter Probabilities and Consequences

A large and significant uncertainty in nuclear winter research concerns fire characteristics. Scientists are focusing on a number of important variables ranging from how much material will burn under a prescribed exchange to the effect of fire-produced toxic chemicals and gases on the surviving environment. They note that the knowledge gained by studying fire characteristics can help computer modelers who need the data to more accurately simulate climatic conditions in a perturbed environment. The following are the more significant components of fire research.

Fire Source
• Combustibility of targets
• How much will burn; for how long?

Smoke Production
• How much smoke is produced?
• What are the smoke characteristics?
• What is the smoke particle size and shape?
• What is the smoke chemical composition?

Plume Characteristics
• How high will it go?
• How much will survive the first few hours?

Studying fire uncertainties is a detailed and lengthy exercise involving several scientific disciplines which are interrelated and dependent on each other. Research is progressing in each of the areas discussed below and is beginning to

Source: Physicians For Social Responsibility

provide computer modelers with valuable data from which they can better simulate atmospheric conditions. Scientists must rely on laboratory experiments, prescribed and/or actual forest fires, and accidental industrial burns to test their calculations. In each case, results must be analyzed and then scaled up to meet the assumed proportions created by a nuclear exchange. The "built-in" unknown of a nuclear weapon produced large-scale fire will always exist, and

scientists can only work towards achieving reliable prob-
abilities of fire and smoke production based on some
assumed range of variables.

Targets—The Source of Fire

Fire source uncertainties relate to the issue of targets
which would remain uncertain until an actual conflict. Scientists assert that the severity of nuclear winter is sensitive to
the quantity of urban/industrial combustible material which
eventually burns. They state that cities are much more combustible than nonurban areas, have higher fuel densities, and
would therefore produce larger amounts of smoke and soot.
Other targets may be situated near industrial sites with large
quantities of petroleum products—a major source of oily,
sooty smoke particles. Scientists, however, can only
postulate about the types of potential targets using
categories such as urban cities, rural areas, or wildlands to
calculate combustibility. Scientists note that developing better data on the detailed fire characteristics of potential areas
would provide valuable information on how much of an area
will burn under a given scenario, how intensely, and for how
long. It would also provide valuable information on how fires
ignite, how many would start in a given area, and how far
they would eventually spread.

Smoke—The Critical Input

Another element of uncertainty is smoke production per
fraction of material that burns. To date, little scientific
research has been done in the area of smoke production and
spreading. The amount of smoke produced depends on the
quantities, types, and distribution of combustible materials
in target zones. Some materials tend to produce relatively little smoke, especially wood that is prevalent in residential
construction. However, other materials such as oil, tar,
asphalt, rubber, plastics and synthetics, which are increasingly common in modern commercial construction, tend to
produce thick black smoke.

Scientists also need to better understand smoke particle
size and shape. Some particles absorb light whereas others
scatter light, depending on their composition. According to
scientists, if smoke particles only scatter sunlight, the

resulting temperature decrease at the earth's surface would not be as severe. Also, they state that smaller smoke particles tend to absorb sunlight more efficiently, resulting in larger temperature reductions. However, scientists need to study further the composition of smoke particles produced by different fuels in large-scale fires. Until then, accurate predictions of how much sunlight will be absorbed and how far temperatures will drop will be difficult to make. How far the predictions can be refined is questionable. Further progress may have to rely on laboratory and small scale fire research requiring considerable extrapolation to simulate the magnitude of fires that would be produced in a nuclear exchange.

Ability to Model Atmospheric Effects is Limited

Studying detailed, complex physical phenomena such as nuclear winter requires sophisticated mathematical models. These models, run in high capacity computers, are deterministic by nature; that is, once the input variables are selected the results are uniquely determined. However, the computer atmospheric models currently used in nuclear winter research are limited in their ability to accurately represent the physical laws of nature and are very much dependent on other research efforts to provide needed data.

Impediments to Computer Modeling

In studying nuclear winter scientists must assume many distinct input variables (i.e. number of weapons used, targets hit, amount of smoke injected into the atmosphere, height of injection, etc.). Computer simulations to date have produced varying results and effects which are limited by the reliability of the input data and constrained by the capabilities of computer software to model dynamic changes in atmospheric conditions and realistically project how long potential effects would last. Until scientists receive more accurate data to apply to their computer climate models and improve their software to simulate atmospheric responses more accurately, modeling results will only show a plausible range of nuclear winter effects under strictly prescribed conditions.

A large impediment to accurately modeling nuclear winter effects is the lack of an analogue (example) from which to

22

compare results. Some scientists in the past have used thunderstorms, volcanic eruptions, day/night and winter/summer changes, large scale forest or urban fires, and even Martian dust storms to help validate their computer atmospheric simulations. However, a nuclear exchange could bring about unprecedented climatic disturbances and there is no analogue which is well suited to test the validity of modeling results. As such, scientific findings will, to some degree, always remain uncertain.

Biological and Agricultural Effects: The Bottom Line of Uncertainty

Beyond the unknowns of how a nuclear war will be conducted and the physical science uncertainties with fire research and climate modeling is the question of the potential effects a nuclear exchange would have on the biological and agricultural environments. Many scientists believe the real long-term consequences of any nuclear crisis would be the potential disruption of ecosystems upon which man is dependent.

Ecosystems consist of the community of plants, animals, and microorganisms that exist in an area (e.g. field, valley, lake, state, continent, etc.) and the physical environment of that community. They depend on the light energy of the sun, which is converted through photosynthesis in green plants into chemical energy that is used by all organisms. The disruption of photosynthesis, scientists conclude, by the reduction of sunlight or temperature drops could have consequences that ultimately cascade through the food chain. Compounding these effects is that after a nuclear war the available supplies of food could be destroyed or contaminated, located in inaccessible areas, or rapidly depleted. In addition, natural ecosystems may not be able to recover in a perturbed environment to resupply the food chain. This presents some important questions which scientists believe need to be addressed. They include:

- What is the effect of sustained low light on plant physiology?
- What would plant stress response be to an unnatural sudden or slow temperature decrease?
- How long would ecosystems, or parts thereof, take to recover?

Research on the potential biological and agricultural implications that could arise from a nuclear winter scenario has been very limited to date. Some scientists and others stated that it is premature to devote significant attention to biological consequences because the assumptions about the environmental and climatic conditions would have to be estimated so broadly as to render the results highly uncertain. But others say that the biological sensitivities to nuclear war are critical to post-war recovery. They believe the potential range of effects warrants studying this issue now in parallel with the physical science research. Also, a view has been expressed that contributions from the biological sciences community can help physical scientists identify or modify priorities in their own research, and that some effort to this end is warranted.

INTRODUCTION

NUCLEAR WINTER AND STRATEGIC POLICY

Publicity surrounding the nuclear winter issue has given rise to speculation and concern over its policy implications. Views on implications range from rhetorical questioning of what nuclear winter adds to the already recognized horrors of nuclear war to views that massive reductions in nuclear arsenals are needed to avoid triggering a nuclear winter should nuclear weapons ever be used. The administration's response to date has essentially been to take a wait-and-see attitude from a policy standpoint, particularly in light of the recognized scientific uncertainties. Others, however, believe that the theory supports changes to some existing policies. But precisely what should be done and when remains unclear. Continued debate and discussion on potential policy implications are needed and should be fostered as a basis for informed decision-making. . . .

Congress Requires Administration to Report on Potential Nuclear Winter Policy Implications

The administration's formal position on nuclear winter policy implications is most clearly stated in a legislatively mandated March 1985 report to the Congress by the Secretary of Defense on "The Potential Effects Of Nuclear

Excerpted from a report by the U.S. Government Accounting Office titled *Nuclear Winter's Uncertainties Surround the Long-Term Effects of Nuclear War,* March, 1986, pp. 26-35.

War On The Climate." Views expressed in that report indicate a cautious approach toward acknowledging policy implications much less considering any changes at this time. Dissatisfied with the report, Congress has required DOD to reassess potential nuclear winter policy implications and provide a new report by March 1, 1986. . . .

DOD's Response

DOD's report, after synopsizing nuclear winter's scientific aspects, concluded that (1) the present uncertainties concerning the effects of nuclear war on the atmosphere preclude considering policy changes at this time and (2) present policies appear adequate. The report avoids the use of the term nuclear winter in favor of such terms as the potential effects of nuclear war on the climate or atmosphere. We use the term nuclear winter in paraphrasing DOD's position solely as a shorthand reference to the theory, and not to infer DOD's endorsement of the theory.

DOD concluded that nuclear winter only strengthens the basic imperative of U.S. national security policy—to prevent nuclear war through a strong deterrence capability.[1] . . .

Policy Issues Frequently Linked With Nuclear Winter

To highlight the range of views on potential policy implications, we have summarized them in terms of the following questions:
• How could nuclear winter affect deterrence?
• How could nuclear winter affect nuclear arsenals and prospects for arms reductions and nonproliferation?
• How could nuclear winter affect warfighting capabilities, targeting, and strategy?
• How could nuclear winter affect crisis stability and control efforts?
• How could nuclear winter affect U.S. civil defense?

[1]This refers to preventing war by showing that U.S. defense capabilities can respond to any level of attack by inflicting unacceptable damage to an aggressor and denying their attainment of war objectives.

How Nuclear Winter Could Affect Deterrence

The goal of U.S. nuclear strategy is to prevent nuclear war by maintaining deterrence. One perspective on the nuclear winter issue is that the possibility it could occur should in itself act to deter a nuclear attack especially if scientific research adds support to the theory that adverse climatic and environmental consequences might rebound to an attacking nation even absent a retaliatory strike. Others express concern that if nuclear winter effects are eventually discounted or reduced significantly, nuclear war could be perceived as less disastrous than previously thought and thus possibly more thinkable. This view seems to ignore the horrible effects of nuclear war which are already recognized. . . .

How Nuclear Winter Could Affect Nuclear Arsenals and Prospects for Arms Reductions and Nonproliferation

Because of concern over nuclear winter, some views at one end of the scale have argued for massive reductions in nuclear weapons, while at the other end, some have expressed the potential need for a new round of weapons development. Some cite reduction in U.S. stockpiles of older weapon systems and the trend toward lower yield, more highly accurate nuclear weapons as being steps in the right direction based on current scientific knowledge. Others see potential impacts on arms reductions negotiations and nonproliferation efforts. . . .

The United States and over 125 other member states (including the U.S.S.R.) are party to a 15-year old Treaty On the Non-Proliferation Of Nuclear Weapons (NPT). The NPT includes among its major provisions an obligation to pursue negotiations in good faith on effective measures leading to cessation of the nuclear arms race and nuclear disarmament. The provision was meant to provide an incentive for non-nuclear nations to commit themselves not to seek, acquire, or manufacture nuclear explosives. It is unclear at this time whether or to what extent the nuclear winter issue will add to any existing concerns or actions by other nations regarding what many see as limited progress towards arms reductions and disarmament. Nor is it clear what, if any, influence

Victims of Hiroshima

they might seek to assert on arms negotiations if it becomes clear these and other nations would no longer be unaffected bystanders to a nuclear conflict between the United States and the Soviet Union.

How Nuclear Winter Could Affect Warfighting Capabilities, Targeting, and Strategy

In the past people have questioned what effect a protracted nuclear conflict would have on warfighting capabilities. The nuclear winter issue adds another dimension to this question and a corollary one of whether command, control, communication, and intelligence (commonly referred to as C³I) functions would be effective in a perturbed environment.

One issue that has stirred considerable discussion involves potential targets in a nuclear conflict, particularly whether, and to what extent, likely targets include or are located in close proximity to urban/industrial areas (cities). DOD's official response to questions on this subject is to the effect that the United States does not target cities. This response does not indicate what their beliefs are regarding the Soviet Union's targeting plans. Also not addressed by

28

this response is to what extent specified targets and objectives in urban/industrial areas would be struck, directly or indirectly, even if cities are not targeted. This is important because of the potential for urban targets to generate and inject greater amounts of smoke and soot particles into the atmosphere. An apparently serious proposal that has been advanced in some of the literature on the subject calls for a U.S./U.S.S.R. bilateral agreement on non-targeting of cities. However, some have questioned the effectiveness of such an agreement since the commitment to its terms could not be verified. . . .

How Nuclear Winter Could Affect Crisis Management and Control Efforts

Crisis management and control efforts are seen by many as safeguards to prevent nuclear war. The potential implications of nuclear winter could provide an incentive to improve these safeguards to make crisis management more efficient and survivable. Such improvements would also reduce both the potential for nuclear weapons use and the possible threat of nuclear winter's adverse environmental and climatic consequences.

During the last 25 years, the United States and U.S.S.R. have concluded some important agreements to facilitate communication between the superpowers to reduce the likelihood of nuclear war. These have included the Hotline Agreement of 1963, the Hotline Modernization Agreement of 1971, the Accidental Measures Agreement of 1971, and the Prevention of Nuclear War Agreement of 1973. In 1983, the administration endorsed four DOD initiatives to improve crisis management. They were to (1) upgrade the hotline for greater speed and for facsimile transmissions, (2) establish a joint military communications link between the Pentagon and Soviet Defense Ministry, (3) improve communications between the government capitals and their respective embassies, and (4) facilitate discussions to resolve terrorist nuclear acts or other unauthorized use of nuclear weapons. The administration has achieved agreement with the Soviet Union on only the first and last initiatives.

The Congress, in enacting the Foreign Relations Authorization Act for fiscal years 1986 and 1987 (the same act which encourages the United States to propose cooperative measures to study the nuclear winter issue with the Soviets) also mandated a detailed executive branch study and evaluation of the U.S. crisis management system, including consideration of the additional steps needed to enhance crisis stability and crisis control capabilities. . . .

How Nuclear Winter Could Affect U.S. Civil Defense

FEMA (Federal Emergency Management Agency) officials indicated they have monitored the nuclear winter issue from a scientific and policy perspective from its inception. Their position, as previously noted, is that scientific knowlege regarding the climatic effects of nuclear explosions has not been developed enough to warrant development of new policies or to change existing policies regarding civil defense. We did not examine U.S. civil defense planning or the adequacy of FEMA's resources to accomplish its mission. We did note, however, a range of views on the potential effect of nuclear winter on civil defense efforts that may provide some perspective for examining future civil defense needs.

One view often publicly expressed is that the United States does not adequately protect against even the immediate effects of nuclear attack. Therefore, it would be unrealistic to think that civil defense programs could be implemented to protect against nuclear winter effects. Another view is that if nuclear winter consequences reach the magnitude suggested by some scientific studies, then it could render useless any attempted civil defense measures. Others say that to the extent scientific research shows reduced levels of effect or a variety of effects and/or severity over space and time, then an argument for contingency planning addressing such factors as food and water, fuel supplies, and delivery systems becomes more convincing.

Conclusions

To date, because of the uncertainty of existing scientific research, the administration has not translated nuclear winter concerns into policy changes. The foregoing discussion of some of the policy implications concerning nuclear winter indicates the difficulties likely to be encountered in trying to sort out the implications and required responses.

EXAMINING COUNTERPOINTS

This activity may be used as an individualized study guide for students in libraries and resource centers or as a discussion catalyst in small group and classroom discussions.

The Point

There are obscenely too many nuclear weapons in the world—both strategic and tactical. They serve no military purpose and place in grave jeopardy not only the nations that have these arsenals but the rest of the peoples on this planet as well. What is urgently needed is bilateral—eventually multilateral—negotiations to bring about massive phased and verifiable reductions in the strategic arsenals of the two superpowers. This should be done in a way that does not, at any stage in the arms reduction, compromise the security of either nation. It ought to be accompanied by a Comprehensive Test Ban Treaty—which is technically and diplomatically the easiest to implement—and, for reasons that I tried to stress in my testimony, a ban on introducing weapons in space. None of these steps requires major technological advances, only political will. (Dr. Carl Sagan in testimony before the Senate Armed Services Committee, October 3, 1985.)

The Counterpoint:

Arms talks help the Soviets because they misleadingly establish them as the coguarantors of world peace. In fact they are the sole threat to it.

Washington has nothing to gain from arms control and plenty to lose. We are told that our allies want it and that many in Congress want it. Yes, but that still does not tell us what military purpose such talks serve.

Considering the aggressive nature of Communism, its history of expansion, the buildup of Soviet arms, and the simultaneous record of Soviet deception and lies, it is fantastic that one should even have to make the case for nuclear superiority; and do so, I might add, with a sense of temerity and isolation. (Tom Bethell, editor of the *American Spectator* from articles in the *New York Times* and the *National Review,* 1986.)

Guidelines

Social issues are usually complex, but often problems become oversimplified in political debates and discussion. Usually a polarized version of social conflict does not adequately represent the diversity of views that surround social conflicts.

1. Examine the counterpoints above. Then write down other possible interpretations of this issue than the two arguments stated in the counterpoints above.
2. How do you interpret the cartoon below?

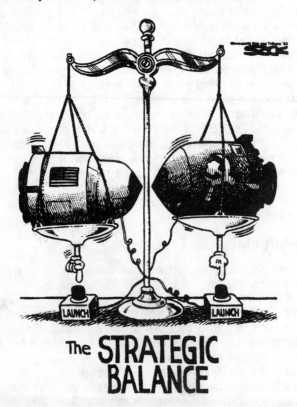

The STRATEGIC BALANCE

Reprinted by permission of the *Minneapolis Star and Tribune.*

CHAPTER 2

NUCLEAR WINTER: IDEAS IN CONFLICT

4   DESTROYING GLOBAL CIVILIZATION
        Carl Sagan and Physicians for Social Responsibilty

5   NUCLEAR WINTER IS IMPROBABLE
        Edward Teller

6   REPORTS ARE GREATLY EXAGGERATED
        George Rathjens

7   BIOLOGICAL EFFECTS OF NUCLEAR WINTER
        Stephen J. Gould

NUCLEAR WINTER: IDEAS IN CONFLICT

Destroying Global Civilization

Carl Sagan and Physicians for Social Responsibility

The first part of this reading is excerpted from a statement by the Physicians for Social Responsibility and the second part is a description by Carl Sagan of how the theory of nuclear winter originated. Dr. Carl Sagan, an astronomer, is one of the scientists who discovered the theory of nuclear winter.

Points to Consider

1. How much explosive power does a small two megaton nuclear weapon possess?
2. How would nuclear explosions affect medical services?
3. What would cause a nuclear winter?
4. What would be the global effects of a nuclear winter?
5. Why might a first strike by an aggressor nation be an act of national suicide by the aggressor nation?

Excerpted from a position paper by Physicians for Social Responsibility and testimony by Carl Sagan before the House Committee on Science and Technology, September 12, 1984.

A large-scale nuclear exchange could mean the extinction of the human race.

COMMENTS BY
PHYSICIANS FOR SOCIAL RESPONSIBILITY

There are now more than 50,000 nuclear weapons deployed in the arsenals of the United States and the Soviet Union—enough to obliterate a *million* Hiroshimas. A *small* strategic warhead with a yield of two megatons (the equivalent of two million tons of TNT) has the explosive power of *all* of the bombs used in the Second World War. Imagine this level of destructiveness compressed into a few seconds and confined to an area 30 to 40 miles across—say *your* city.

In the wake of such an explosion, there would be no effective medical response. The number of local burn victims alone would exceed by many times the number of intensive care units in all of the United States. Many of your area's doctors and nurses would be among the dead and injured and most of your local hospitals would be destroyed or extensively damaged. Even if such care were possible and enough physicians were willing to enter a highly radioactive area, there would be no means to transport physicians to the victims or the victims to the physicians. And even if transport were available, the absence of support personnel, equipment, beds, diagnostic and X-ray facilities, blood, plasma and drugs would make their task impossible. But in addition to having to treat the monumental number of burned, lacerated and irradiated victims, control of epidemic illness would become an insuperable problem, not to mention the logistics required to remove several million corpses. Moreover, a nuclear attack on your city would likely mean hundreds of simultaneous nuclear detonations elsewhere. Practically speaking, no help would be forthcoming from the outside world.

For the past five years, Physicians for Social Responsibility has presented this grim warning to millions of Americans: nuclear war, even a "limited" one as described above, would result in death, injury and disease on a scale that has no precedent in human history. Through expert testimony, we have labored to demonstrate the effect of nuclear weapons and show that medical "disaster planning" for nuclear war would be meaningless. But now in the face of new evidence on the *aftermath* of nuclear war—the "nuclear winter"—we realize that the prognosis for man's survival is far graver than we had ever believed. We knew we would be helpless to save dying people by the millions. Now we know that after a nuclear war, we would be powerless to save most life on this planet.

The Days After: The Nuclear Winter

A consensus of more than 100 scientists at a recent conference on "The World After Nuclear War" revealed that a large-scale nuclear exchange could mean the extinction of the human race.

This assessment, presented by Cornell astronomer Carl Sagan and Stanford biologist Paul Ehrlich, was based on the emerging data about the climatic, biological and environmental effects of a nuclear war. The study had its origins in data collected by the space vehicle Mariner 9, when it explored the planet Mars in 1971. The probe found that dust storms over that planet created sharp temperature differences between the atmosphere and the planet's surface and took months to settle. When conference biologists and atmospheric physicists applied their findings to planet Earth, the results were horrifying.

Using computer models of the likely effects of the dust and smoke created by nuclear war, the study selected as the most likely war scenario an exchange involving 5,000 megatons, or about one-third of the currently existing nuclear weapons. Within weeks after such an exchange, soot, smoke and dust from nuclear fires and groundbursts would reduce the amount of sunlight at ground level to a few percent of normal. An unbroken gloom would persist for a considerable time over the Northern Hemisphere. For the next months, the light filtering through this pall might not be adequate to sustain photosynthesis, the process by which plants convert sunlight to food. The lack of sunlight would create a harsh "nuclear winter" with temperatures dropping to 25 degrees Celsius (minus thirteen degrees Fahrenheit) and stay below freezing for months, even as a result of a

Most Shocking Finding

But the most shocking finding of the entire study was that "an epoch of cold and dark almost as severe as in the 5,000 megaton case" could be triggered by a war involving 100 megatons of explosive power, one percent of superpower arsenals and a fiftieth the size of the base case. No prior analysis had ever presumed the possibility of such serious damage from so small a nuclear exchange.

Paul Ehrlich and Carl Sagan, *Not Man Apart,* December, 1983

summer war. If the nuclear exchange occurred in spring or summer, virtually all crops would be destroyed in the Northern Hemisphere. Most of the human survivors and animals would starve or die of thirst as surface waters froze over.

Because radioactive debris in huge quantities, an estimated 225 billion tons over a few days, would be carried through the atmosphere, exposure to radioactive fallout would be much more widespread than predicted by earlier estimates. Moreover, high yield nuclear explosions would greatly weaken the ozone layer which screens the earth from excessive amounts of ultraviolet rays. This could have a fatal impact on microorganisms in the soil as well as aquatic life. Meanwhile, urban fires set off by the nuclear blasts would generate large amounts of deadly toxins by vaporizing the large quantities of synthetic chemicals stored in cities. Forest fires would rage through dead trees. Plagues of insect pests—the animal life best equipped to survive the disaster—would damage remaining food stuffs and spread disease. Immunity to disease would decline rapidly. Epidemics would be rampant, especially after the billion or so unburied bodies began to thaw.

The cold, the dark and the intense radioactivity together lasting for months, would represent a severe assault on our civilization and our species. Civil and sanitary services would be wiped out. Medical facilities, drugs and the basic means for relieving the vast human suffering would be unavailable. Any but the most elaborate shelters would be useless, quite apart from the question of what good it would do to emerge a few months later. Moreover the combined influences of these "severe and simultaneous" stresses on life are likely to produce even more adverse consequences—biologists call them synergisms—that we are not yet wise enough to understand.

As Carl Sagan concluded: "Many biologists, considering the nuclear winter that these calculations described, believe they carry somber implications for life on Earth. Many species of plants and animals would become extinct. Vast numbers of surviving humans would starve to death. *The delicate ecological relations that bind together organisms on Earth in a fabric of mutual dependency would be torn, perhaps irreparably. There is little question that our global civilization would be destroyed. The human population would be reduced to prehistoric levels, or less. Life for any survivors would be extremely hard. And there seems to be a real possibility of the extinction of the human species.*"

In sum, there are no sanctuaries from nuclear war. The interconnecting web of systems that sustain life on the planet would be shattered. A nuclear attack would be suicide for the nation that launched it, even if there was no retaliatory strike. "Now," said one of the many Russian physicists who contributed to the study, "the whole of the earth and human civilization itself are held hostage." Can a nuclear war be won? As Dr. Sagan has said, "The ashes of communism and capitalism will be indistinguishable."

COMMENTS BY CARL SAGAN

The first step on the road to uncovering nuclear winter came in 1971 when the Mariner 9 spacecraft was in orbit around Mars, and examined for many months a global dust storm which had the interesting property of warming the upper atmosphere considerably and cooling the surface of Mars considerably. That was a suggestion that fine particles in a planetary atmosphere can heat the atmosphere, cool the surface and drive from the heating of the atmosphere the fine particles over the Equator into the opposite hemisphere.

38

NUCLEAR WAR PLANNING ROOM

" THE PROBLEM IN GETTING THE PRESIDENT AIRBORNE BEFORE AN ATTACK IS THAT
AFTER THE ATTACK THERE WON'T BE ANYPLACE TO LAND ! "

We were able to calculate what the effects would be; found that they were comparable to what was observed, and later used that computational armamentarium to calculate what the consequences for the Earth's climate would be of large volcanic explosions which characteristically cool the Earth by fraction of a degree—not from dust, but mainly liquid sulfuric acid droplets punched into the stratosphere.

Then my colleagues, but not myself, addressed the issue of the question of the massive floral and faunal extinction 65 million years ago, which led to the extinction of the dinosaurs and many other species, and which is now widely but not universally thought to be due to the impact on the Earth of an asteroid or cometary nucleus, the projection of a large cloud of fine silicate particles cooling and darkening the Earth and that is generally thought to have been the event that led to a lot of grief for a lot of inhabitants of the Earth at the cretaceous/tertiary transition 65 million years ago.

TTAPS Group

Only then did we—the names of the authors are Turco, Toon, Ackerman, Pollack and myself—briefly called the TTAPS group, a not inappropriate acronym considering the nature of the results—only then—did we think of seriously working on the nuclear war issue. We were thinking at first only of dust. There was then an important paper by Crutzen and Birks which talked about soot. They talked mainly about soot from the burning of forests in a nuclear war. They talked about substantial darkening of the Northern Hemisphere, but did not talk about cooling.

We then calculated for a wide range of cases, some 50 different scenarios and variations of uncertain parameters over their plausible range, what the consequences of various nuclear wars might be, and found to our great surprise, because this was—or at least should have been—a well-studied area, that a large number of scenarios yielded absolutely catastrophic results, locally, hemisphere-wide and probably globally.

The work was presented at a number of forums, reviewed by a very large number of scientists and published in the journal, Science. There have been a number of confirmatory calculations subsequently. Vladimir Aleksandrov of the Computing Centre of the Soviet Academy of Sciences, who is here, did the first global circulation model on nuclear winter. Alan Robock of the University of Maryland, who is here, has done an important recent study suggesting that the effects would persist considerably longer than we calculated in the TTAPS paper.

Let me stress that there necessarily are uncertainties in any calculation of this sort. Nuclear war is not a problem that is amenable to experimental verification, or at least not more than once, and we do not wish to perform the experiment. The results, therefore, have to depend upon laboratory and field measurements of single nuclear weapons explosions and fires set intentionally and unintentionally, laboratory results and theoretical calculations involving some of the most difficult aspects of classical physics, hydrodynamics of a complex weather system.

There are differences of opinion, although I must say that the great bulk of the published work suggests that the original TTAPS results are somewhere in the neighborhood

Ollie Harrington

"General, with ten of these babies you can blow up the whole planet, but we're prepared to give you a very special price if you order 100."

of what might happen, and curiously enough, this also seems to be the opinion of the Department of Defense. In testimony before the Joint Economic Committee last July 12, Mr. Richard Wagner, Assistant to Defense Secretary Weinberger, said: "There would be a nuclear winter even if there was an exchange at comparatively low yields."

The fact that the Department of Defense takes this seriously is welcome news. It doesn't mean that they're right; the Department of Defense has been mistaken in the past and doubtless will be mistaken in the future, but I stress this convergence of opinion to indicate that a wide variety of different points of view seem to agree that this is something very serious.

There are a number of effects that have been identified which tend to ameliorate the consequences as discussed in the TTAPS results and a number of effects which have been identified which tend to make them worse. It is my opinion and the opinion of my colleagues, that in balance, the

TTAPS results are, in fact, conservative, and that—especially on the duration of nuclear war, of nuclear winter—would probably be considerably longer than the few months that we calculated in our paper.

The Consequences

There are a range of aspects of the problem that have not been examined and which tend to make things worse. Multiburst phenomena, for example: one nuclear explosion propelling the debris from the previous nuclear explosion well up into the stratosphere; tactical nuclear weapons, of which there are only 35,000 in the world, none of which have been involved in the previous scenarios; the kind of feedbacks involving sea ice and increased snow that Allan Robock has identified, which tend to make the effects longer; the production of toxic gases from the burning of synthetics in modern cities; and even more dire possibilities.

Clearly, it's important to narrow the range of uncertainty, especially because there are a set of very serious possible implications for policy and strategy and doctrine if nuclear winter turns out to have even a small chance of being as severe as we say it is. And this includes the very interesting idea that first strikes are self-deterring because the attacked nation need not lift a finger to protect itself or defend itself and the aggressor nation will be destroyed by the cloud of soot and smoke that circulates back to the aggressor nation. It implies that crisis relocation and civilian shelters are even more bankrupt ideas than before nuclear winter. It suggests that nations in parts of the world far distant from the conflict, with no particular role in the quarrel between the antagonists might be utterly destroyed without a single nuclear weapon falling on their territories, and therefore, the stake of other nations in what the United States and the Soviet Union choose to do with the world would have risen significantly. . . .

The consequences of nuclear winter are so severe that even if there were a tiny chance that this was right, you would want to be sure you had done the very best job you could. I believe that no matter what is done, there will be lingering uncertainties and we will have to—as often is the case in policy matters—deal with a circumstance where we do not understand everything.

NUCLEAR WINTER: IDEAS IN CONFLICT

NUCLEAR WINTER
IS IMPROBABLE

Edward Teller

Dr. Edward Teller was among the group of U.S. scientists under the direction of Robert Oppenheimer, who developed the first atomic weapon that was dropped on Hiroshima and Nagasaki.

Points to Consider

1. What points of agreement does the author discuss?
2. How does the danger of nuclear winter differ from the danger of radiation fallout and ozone depletion after a nuclear explosion?
3. Why is the possibility of nuclear winter uncertain?
4. What should be done to avoid a nuclear winter?

Excerpted from testimony by Edward Teller before the House Committee on Science and Technology, September 12, 1984.

The following arguments will show that the uncertainties connected with nuclear winter are exceedingly great. The same arguments will also indicate that the nuclear winter recently sketched in the mass media is improbable.

In a serious and vital debate, it is most important to emphasize the points on which agreement exists as well as the limitations of these agreements. In discussing the present subject, one should state with all possible emphasis that the avoidance of nuclear war, indeed the avoidance of any serious war, may not be just the most important issue of our time, but is surpassed in importance by essentially none other. There are, however, widely varying and indeed mutually contradictory proposals concerning the way in which such wars may best be avoided. This statement is made to avoid misunderstandings concerning the spirit of the following arguments; in itself, it has limited bearing on the more technical issues that will follow.

The second point of basic agreement is that "nuclear winter" is an important topic. The possibility of widespread temperature changes following a nuclear attack should be clarified in every possible way, including the question of whether large-scale destructive effects are probable. There are some who claim that nuclear war will be probably followed by a nuclear winter. There are even those who assert that all scientists agree to the assertion that a dire nuclear winter would be a practically unavoidable consequence of a large-scale nuclear war. The following arguments will show in the first place that the uncertainties connected with nuclear winter are exceedingly great. The same arguments will also indicate that the nuclear winter recently sketched in the mass media is improbable. . . .

Approximately two years ago a serious consequence of nuclear war started to occupy the limelight. This is the influence of the non-radioactive materials distributed in the atmosphere by the nuclear explosion upon the climate. This influence is due to a lesser degree to dust, to a greater degree to smoke. Both tend to reduce solar radiation received on the surface of the earth; if this reduction is sufficiently large and prolonged, it may bring about what is now known as "nuclear winter". . . .

In 1982 Crutzen and Birks proposed that a serious effect on the atmosphere could be caused by the smoke from forest fires which not only scatter sunlight but actually significantly absorb it. In 1983 Turco, et. al (TTAPS) argued that smoke generated in fires from bombed cities and possibly oil refineries would give even greater effects. Based on this paper, Dr. Carl Sagan stated on numerous occasions that, following even a relatively small exchange of nuclear weapons, temperatures between latitudes 30 and 70 of the Northern Hemisphere would drop to values near 40 degrees Fahrenheit below the freezing point, causing great damage to all life and subsequent crop failures that would have further disastrous effects. He also argued that the smoke may well become distributed over the whole globe and that the survival of many species, including our own, would be endangered. While it is generally recognized that details of the process are still uncertain and deserve much more study, Dr. Sagan nevertheless has taken the position that the whole scenario is so robust that there can be little doubt about its main conclusions.

Therefore we have now reached a point where the introduction of a new world-wide consequence of nuclear war is currently believed by many to lead to deleterious effects even greater than the indubitable horrors likely to fall upon the combatant nations.

Uncertainties Concerning the Nuclear Winter

The danger of a nuclear winter differs from fallout and ozone depletion in an essential way. The nuclear winter depends on meteorological phenomena that involve much more detailed considerations and calculations than either the questions of fallout or ozone depletion, even though the latter requires the understanding of a complicated sequence of more than a hundred chemical reactions in the atmosphere. Therefore, to obtain reliable answers on temperature changes in the atmosphere in the case of the nuclear winter scenario will take a longer time and require more expenditure of thought and dollars than the elucidation of the other two dangers that have been noted.

Preventing War

The issue here is that depicting defense as futile, insane and suicidal invites nuclear war; indeed, foments it. That such a war would be horrible is self-evident without the sermons by pampered profs like Ehrlich and Sagan who have seen the horrors of war only in comic strips and on the boob tube. They are undercutting those who want to prevent war; and the only way of preventing it is to have the will to resist and the capacity to win.

Petr Beckmann, *Access to Energy,* December, 1983

This complicating factor does not in itself exclude the statement that the effect of smoke on world-wide temperatures may be robust and that the actual occurrence and the intensity of a nuclear winter could be predicted with confidence. However, detailed considerations of all processes, together with the uncertainties connected with them, lead to the conclusion, as will be shown below, that the argument for the occurrence of a nuclear winter, instead of being robust, is indeed quite inconclusive. . . .

Let us now turn to the argument of Dr. Sagan which is adduced to prove that nuclear winter is practically unavoidable. This argument is that the smoke-loaded air, being heated by the sunlight, will attain sufficient buoyancy to rise toward the tropopause where the normal temperature of air is in the neighborhood of minus 50 to 60°C. The presence of this smoke would make itself felt over broad areas for about one month and the temperature of the air in this region would be raised in a remarkable and understandable manner to about plus 5°C while the surface temperature would be rapidly dropping. Thus, instead of the usual decrease of air temperature with increasing altitude, we would have an increasing temperature with altitude over the earth's land masses, called in meteorology an inversion. In such regions of inversion, the buoyancy mechanism that acts on rising air masses does not occur and water condensation and rain does not develop. Thus, Dr. Sagan infers that the smoke would persist in the upper atmosphere and, in spite of the presence of much more water vapor, shielding of the earth's surface from the sunlight could persist over long periods of time.

Actually, this mechanism for cooling of the earth's surface is effective only over land, while over the oceans where warm water is continually supplied from below for periods of many months, the temperature at the surface would remain essentially unchanged. Thus, over the surface of the earth unusually great temperature differences would be established between continents and oceans if a nuclear winter were ever to commence. These would probably result in violent air motions, widespread turbulence, and large, continuing rain storms, points mentioned even by Dr. Sagan and his colleagues (though not taken into account at all in their calculations).

By David Seavey, USA TODAY

Copyright, 1986 *USA TODAY*. Reprinted with permission.

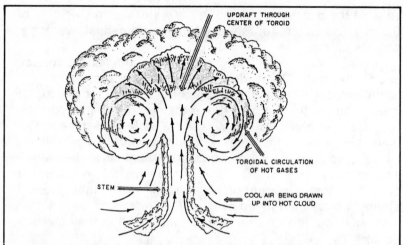

Cutaway showing an artist's conception of the chimney-like airflow following the detonation of a nuclear weapon near the earth's surface. Since the detonation occurs near the surface, the very hot fireball vaporizes material from the target and the nearby surrounding area. In addition, the sudden differential heating of clumps of earth, rock, and sand by the hot fireball, followed by the passage of a violent shock wave, creates large amounts of dust in the target area. Much of this material is swept from the ground by very intense afterwinds.

As these winds carry the dust aloft, the rotating toroidal air flow within the rising hot fireball draws the dust into the fireball's center and mixes it with cooling radioactive bomb debris. Within the fireball, some of the cooling bomb debris will condense into very fine droplets, but much of it will instead "plate-out" onto these dust particles. Because many of these particles are relatively large, they can fall to the ground over periods of minutes or hours, transporting substantial amounts of radioactive bomb debris with them.

Source: House Committee on Science and Technology

There is reason to believe that the warm wet air over the oceans will rise only to a fraction of the altitude of the postulated smoke layer over the land areas. The primary cause of the storms is, therefore, concentrated in the lower part of the atmosphere. However, it is well known that storms and the associated turbulent air motion quite often extend far above the region of the original cause of the storm. Thus, water may be convected into the smoke-laden air layer over the continental margins, rain out the smoke, and thus prevent uniform distribution or long-term persistence of the smoke. One should also note that rain removing smoke from extensive areas while leaving it relatively untouched in other areas would give the smoke layer a patchy nature. This in turn would bring about additional large temperature differences which will further drive the atmospheric processes that will rain out the smoke. Rain out of large smoke layers may thereby proceed in an accelerating fashion.

A possibly more important doubt arises from the consideration that, according to every detailed calculation, the world-wide mixing and lofting of the smoke and the onset of nuclear winter takes about two weeks to develop. During this period, as noted above, most—perhaps virtually all—of the smoke is apt to be caught at lower altitudes and rained out there. By ignoring these several basic points, one might be led to the belief that one's argument for nuclear winter driven by persistent smoke is robust.

Initially, some smoke, particularly the strongly absorbing carbon particles resulting from oil fires, may be water-repellant. This property, however, changes after an exposure to air. Wood fires, moreover, appear to produce water-attracting particles even initially. Therefore, there is no reason to expect that rainout of all types of smoke particles would not occur. . . .

It is not contended that the arguments given above disprove the possibililty of a nuclear winter. It is believed, however, that the reasons for very significant uncertainty are considerable in number and in weight. . . .

Considering all the uncertainties enumerated, it seems that the arguments for a nuclear winter would be more justly described not as "robust" but rather as "quite dubious".

Countermeasures

Since the possibility of a nuclear winter has not been conclusively excluded, the question arises what should be done about it. The first and most obvious measure is increased research which will help to decide the question. . . .

In addition to arguing for more knowledge, I agree with Dr. Sagan that serious thought should be given to the avoidance of nuclear winter, even though I firmly hope that any nuclear war can be avoided and even though I believe that the development of a nuclear winter is far from certain under any circumstances. In this connection, I would like to quote a most outstanding physicist, Freeman Dyson, who in the *New Yorker* has recently given much serious thought to questions connected with nuclear war. While Dr. Sagan says that the possibility of a nuclear winter will be tested at most only once, Dyson takes a very different view. He says, "The effects of the first nuclear war might be severe enough not to exterminate mankind but to leave our species in some sense incurably insane. Hatred and suffering on an unparalleled scale might lock us into a cyclical pattern of war and rearmament and revenge which would in the end make our planet uninhabitable."

I believe that the most grim consequences of a nuclear war are, indeed, not the material damage and not even the enormous loss of human life, but the probable spiritual damage to the fabric of human civilization extending over the whole world. In this I thoroughly agree with Professor Dyson.

But there is an even more important point. If anything approaching a nuclear winter should occur, widespread crop failures might be the most severe reason for human suffering and death. Methods for preservation of appropriate foods should be developed and major food stocks should be established worldwide. This may not only help in the survival of our own people, but it might save many lives abroad. Indeed, doing so would be a step away from the "incurable insanity" that Professor Dyson has mentioned.

In his article in *Foreign Affairs,* Dr. Sagan suggested reduction of nuclear weapons which in two decades or a little more might eliminate the danger of nuclear winter. We have tried, almost since the end of World War II, to obtain Russian agreement to nuclear arms control. I believe that the arguments for Soviet adherence to any arms control agreement are less than robust. I am also sure that countermeasures of which we ourselves are capable can be executed in a few years rather than the period of decades suggested by Dr. Sagan. These methods include active defense, civil defense and food storage.

If we can destroy incoming missiles before they can set our cities, refineries, or forests afire, not only will nuclear winter be eliminated or at least made far less likely, but we may have also saved our lives and our society. Such a defense is feasible through use of antiballistic missiles and possibly other methods. Indeed, the very possibility of effective strategic defense may serve as a powerful deterrent to nuclear war.

NUCLEAR WINTER:
IDEAS IN CONFLICT

REPORTS ARE
GREATLY EXAGGERATED

George Rathjens

Dr. George Rathjens is a professor of political science at the Massachusetts Institute of Technology in Cambridge, Massachusetts.

Points to Consider

1. What kind of statement can be made about nuclear winter?
2. How is the TTAPS study evaluated?
3. How might government react to the possibility of nuclear winter?
4. What actions might be taken about nuclear winter by nations that would never be likely to be attacked by nuclear weapons?

Excerpted from testimony by George Rathjens before the House Committee on Interior and Insular Affairs, March 14, 1985.

But above all, I would emphasize that the problem of estimating the seriousness of "nuclear winter" is completely dominated by uncertainty.

I welcome the opportunity to join with you in this discussion of "nuclear winter", particularly because clarification about the nature, likelihood and implications of the phenomenon is mostly sorely needed. This is because reporting has been bad, abetted, I am sorry to say, by some careless, even irresponsible, statements by some members of the scientific community. Thus, the public, and I dare say many members of Congress, have been led to believe that in the event of a large scale nuclear war there would develop a pall of smoke and dust that would spread over much of the northern hemisphere—perhaps all of it and possibly extending even into the southern hemisphere as well—and that this would so reduce the incidence of sunlight at the earth's surface that the result would be sub-freezing temperatures for at least weeks over large areas, even in the event of a war's occurring in summer. There would be dramatic changes in weather patterns, massive crop failures and destruction of biological species, including possibly man. Much of this could happen, but there is no basis for claiming that it would happen or even that it is likely.

To a large extent such dire prognostications have their bases in a study reported in Science magazine in December 1983, now commonly referred to as the TTAPS study after the initials of its authors. It was a pioneering effort deserving of great credit, but it was apparent at the time that because of the uncertainties in critical assumptions and simplifications in modelling, its estimates of diminution in temperatures could only be regarded as illustrative.

TTAPS Study

Since the publication of TTAPS, much additional work has been done, and the National Academy of Sciences and more recently the Department of Defense have reviewed the state of knowledge about the phenomenon. Two points from these reviews deserve to be highlighted: (1) "nuclear winter" could happen; (2) the uncertainties—only some of which are likely to be resolved or significantly narrowed in the next few years—are so many and so large as to preclude making meaningful predictions about its seriousness. Temperatures over continental land masses could drop by tens of degrees and remain well below normal for weeks or months but just as plausibly the effects could be within the range of normal year to year variations, i.e. so small as to be scarcely noticeable.

Secretary Weinberger's report highlights the additional point, with which I strongly agree, that there are a number of problems in the TTAPS work that mean that its estimates of effects should be much reduced. To give but two examples, TTAPS assumes that smoke from fires initiated by nuclear war is spread instantaneously and uniformly over the whole of the northern hemisphere, when in fact such spreading would likely take weeks, during which much, albeit a highly uncertain fraction, of the smoke would be removed, and it does not take account quantitatively of the warming effect on continental land masses of the movement of air from over the oceans and from the tropics. Correcting for such omissions would lead to several-fold reductions in the magnitude of effects estimated in TTAPS. When corrections for such deficiencies are compounded with the many other sources of uncertainty that are important in estimating "nuclear winter" effects—the amounts of smoke produced, its soot content, the height to which it rises, and its persistence, and with those associated with the circulation of air masses—I believe that diminutions in temperature are likely to be in the range of zero to five degrees centigrade, not tens of degrees, as TTAPS and some other reports suggest. But above all, I would emphasize that the problem of estimating the seriousness of "nuclear winter" is completely dominated by uncertainty.

Government Reaction

I should like now to turn to the questions of how governments should react to the "discovery" of "nuclear winter", aside from perhaps supporting research which might reduce the range of uncertainties about it. Let me assume for the moment that the effects would be as serious as those suggested in TTAPS.

Doves and nuclear disarmers—and I count myself among them—would argue for great efforts to reduce nuclear stockpiles and for less dependence on nuclear weapons as instruments of policy, even if the price were greater dependence on conventional arms. But believing we should be moving in these directions anyway, I discount the argument very heavily. No one should be misled that "nuclear winter" is going to make nuclear war a much more horrifying prospect for people of the NATO or Warsaw Pact countries than it would be, nuclear winter aside. Any war that could conceivably produce serious nuclear winter effects would likely be utterly catastrophic in any case.

For many others, including most of those responsible for military planning and operations and for various aspects of our nuclear weapons programs, acceptance of "nuclear winter" as a significant consequence of nuclear war could have other effects. One might expect greater emphasis on improving the accuracy of weapons delivery, on replacing those of high yield with those of lower yield, on fuzing weapons for surface rather than air bursts, even recognizing that the last change would mean more fall-out, and that all these changes—except possibly the first—might imply a larger stockpile. It has also been suggested that the prospect of nuclear winter would induce greater caution—at least in the late spring and summer when "nuclear winter" effects would be most significant—in military operations that might lead to escalation to "nuclear winter" levels. But there is the other side of the coin: there could be a greater impetus to use nuclear weapons on a limited scale, based on the belief that the "nuclear winter" prospect would help deter escalation. (I would discount both of these arguments.)

Weapons Programs

Finally, there are the arguments of the Administration, exemplified in Secretary Weinberger's recent statement, that the prospects of "nuclear winter" justify increased support for weapons programs that it claims will reduce the likelihood of nuclear war and/or will lead to arms reduction. Additionally, the Administration has suggested that "nuclear winter" makes its Strategic Defense Initiative more impor-

54

No Possibility for Extinction

"A Simmering Scientific Debate Thaws Nuclear Winter Theory," by Richard Mackenzie, Insight weekly mag., 21Ap86. This layman's article updates the controversy over whether a large nuclear war would cause the freezing out of humanity.

Basically, more sophisicated studies than the one in 1983 by Carl Sagan and Co. are concluding that nuclear war's effects "would not be nearly as severe as the original calculations showed," according to National Center for Atmospheric Research scientist, Stanley Thompson. "They predicted a real possibility of human extinction. The new conclusions show that possibility does not exist."

A review in *Understanding Defense,* April, 1986

---

tant. I buy the logic of these arguments, but I do not buy the Administrations's conclusions because I do not buy its premises. It is unlikely that going ahead with its various weapons programs will make nuclear war less likely or lead to significant arms reduction—I think quite the contrary— and there is not the slightest reason to believe that the SDI would lead to fewer weapons landing in areas where fires might be ignited. Again, the result is likely to be quite the contrary: each side is likely to over-react to its adversary's defense initiatives, the net result being more offensive weapons on both sides and probably more delivered in the event of war than if the defense initiatives had not been undertaken in the first place. (This leads to a general observation about Secretary Weinberger's report: good as the first two sections are, the last is most unsatisfactory, and, as I understand it, not responsive to the Congressional request which led to it.)

Conclusion

My last point: how should the governments of nations not likely to be directly attacked react to the prospect of "nuclear winter"? Many might hope to escape the effects of a NATO-Warsaw Pact nuclear war relatively unscathed but for the possible effects of "nuclear winter". For them, hedging against "nuclear winter" through the stockpiling of food and fuel and the provision of adequate shelter could make a lot of sense—a lot more for them than for the United States or the Soviet Union—provided "nuclear winter" seemed severe and reasonably likely. But there would be a cost in such hedging, just as there is in buying any other kind of insurance, and the cost may be an excruciatingly painful one to bear for many of the poorer countries of the world—a cost not worth paying if there is just a remote chance of severe "nuclear winter".

I am driven to conclude that when account is taken of the uncertainties that attach to the "nuclear winter" phenomenon and the likelihood that the most popular estimates are greatly exaggerated, policy changes by any government based on it would be premature. Certainly, it would be unwise to take actions simply on the assumption that it is prudent to assume the worst. That would be all right if there were no cost to be incurred in doing so, but that is not the way of the world.

NUCLEAR WINTER: IDEAS IN CONFLICT

BIOLOGICAL EFFECTS OF NUCLEAR WINTER

Stephen J. Gould

Dr. Stephen J. Gould is a professor of geology at Harvard University in Cambridge, Massachusetts.

Points to Consider

1. How and why has nuclear winter happened in the past?
2. What are the "three general principles of biological systems" and how might they be related to nuclear war?
3. What could be the long term biological effects of nuclear winter?
4. Why would the result of nuclear war victory by any one nation be the ultimate empty victory?

Excerpted from testimony by Stephen Jay Gould before the House Subcommittee on Natural Resources, September 12, 1984.

Indeed, the experiment of nuclear winter has probably been made upon our earth, perhaps often.

Moses terrified Pharoah with a pall over Egypt: "He sent a thick darkness over all the land, even darkness which might be felt." But Moses' plague lasted only three days. The much longer darkness of nuclear winter with its associated set of consequences, including plummeting temperatures, increased radiation, fires, and enhanced chemical pollution of atmosphere and surface waters, has made the prospect of nuclear war even more frightening than terrified humanity had previously imagined.

Scientific Methods

Some critics have charged that nuclear winter is too uncertain a phenomenon to merit much serious study: after all, the experiment has not (thank goodness) been tried, and science relies on repeatable test. I would make a response leading to the conclusion that more attention and effort must be devoted to this new and realistic threat. . . .

Past Nuclear Winters

Indeed, the experiment of nuclear winter has probably been made upon our earth, perhaps often. The geological record is punctuated by events of mass extinction, perhaps occurring at regular intervals of 26 million years, and wiping out, in the worst case, as many as 95 percent of marine invertebrate species. The causes of mass extinction have, until recently, been the greatest unsolved problem in paleontology. But, since 1980, we have developed evidence, in the form of chemical signatures incorporated in the sediments at extinction boundaries, that at least the most famous of all such events—the Cretaceous dying that wiped out dinosaurs along with some 50 percent of all recorded species—was a complex result of impact by comet or asteroid. The "killing scenario" for such an extinction, developed by Luis Alvarez and his coworkers, invokes a cloud of dust, lofted by the impact, that made the earth so cold and dark that most life perished—in other words, the same phenomenon as nuclear winter. . . .

Models for Nuclear Winter

I shall not comment upon the physical models for nuclear winter developed by my colleagues except to say that I am impressed both with the convergence of basic results reached by several independent simulations performed both in America and in the Soviet Union, and by the substantial agreement about their plausibility and importance reached by so many distinguished scientists, representing a complete spectrum of political attitudes by the way, at meetings arranged to study the results prior to their publication in *Science* magazine on December 23, 1983. Nuclear winter is not the fanciful conjecture of a few, but the result of a remarkable convergence among scientists throughout the world and representing such varied concerns as mass extinction in paleontology, the study of planetary atmospheres, the geology of impacts, atmospheric physics, and global climatic modelling. Rarely has any scientific study been subjected to such widespread scrutiny before publication.

Biological results are vastly more complicated and subject to uncertainty than the physical effects that yielded the basic model of nuclear winter. I will not, therefore, enumerate specific predictions. What we can say, virtually for certain, is that the biological impact will be severe, perhaps irreversibly disastrous (as in the mass extinctions of our geological record. . . .

Biological Results

Three general principles of biological systems engender the uncertainty of specific prediction while leading to the general conviction that biological effects of nuclear winter might be immediate and severe. First, the complexity of interactions. Biological systems contain more complex and interacting components than any other piece of nature. Impacts upon one species or local population may propagate up and down food chains and through ecosystems in waves of increasing severity. If we lose much oceanic phytoplankton through suppression of photosynthesis by low light levels of nuclear winter, we may impact the entire

ecosystem of the sea (since the microscopic plankton lie at
the base of marine food chains), with disastrous effects
upon human fisheries.

Second, the small tolerance of certain biological systems,
particularly those artificially maintained by human interven-
tion. Some (though not all) biological systems are well
buffered by evolutionary history against environmental fluc-
tuations (though not necessarily to the unexperienced effects of nuclear winter). But many biological systems most
crucial to human life, the agriculture of major cereal grains
in particular, are artificially maintained by necessary,
massive and continuous human input. These might collapse
completely under the assault of nuclear winter. Most cereal
fields are unstable monocultures, often grown at the edges
of ecological possibility, made of genetically uniform stocks
(therefore unusually susceptible to disease), and dependent
upon inputs of fertilization and irrigation that would almost
surely be cut off after nuclear exchange.

Third, synergisms, or, in technical parlance, "non-additive
interactions." We cannot, in assessing the impact of disaster
upon natural systems, simply add up the predictable effect
upon each component separately in order to measure the
response of the whole. Bad plus bad need not yield twice as
bad, but often many times worse. The intense radiation of a
nuclear war, for example, might produce by mutation a new
and potent agent of microbial disease. The effect of such a
vector might then be heightened by several other impacts of
radiation: general weakness of organisms by radiation
sickness and particular suppression of immune systems that
might otherwise fight disease.

Long Term Impact

We must distinguish between two types, or scales, of biological effect for nuclear winter: the immediate increment of human suffering and long-term impacts upon ecosystems (including extinctions). Most uncertainties involve the second category of long-term effects, and these potential results are admittedly more spectacular. But effects in the first category—immediate increment of human suffering—are much clearer and more than enough in themselves to justify our deep concern.

Although long-term effects are so hard to predict, I might simply cite in toto the last section, labelled Conclusions, from the original paper written by 20 biologists and published as a companion piece to the original TTAPS report on nuclear winter.

Conclusions (from TTAPS companion paper)

The predictions of climatic changes are quite robust, so that qualitatively the same types of stresses would ensue from a limited war of 500 MT or less in which cities were targeted as from a larger scale nuclear war of 10,000 MT. Essentially, all ecosystem support services would be severely impaired. We emphasize that survivors, at least in the Northern Hemisphere, would face extreme cold, water shortages, lack of food and fuel, heavy burdens of radiation and pollutants, disease, and severe psychological stress—all in twilight or darkness.

The possibility exists that the darkened skies and low temperatures would spread over the entire planet. Should this occur, a severe extinction event could ensue, leaving a highly modified and biologically depauperate Earth. Species extinction could be expected for most tropical plants and animals, and for most terrestrial vertebrates of north temperate regions, a large number of plants, and numerous freshwater and some marine organisms.

It seems unlikely, however, that even in these circumstances, Homo sapiens would be forced to extinction immediately. Whether any people would be able to persist for long in the face of highly modified

biological communities; novel climates; high levels of
radiation; shattered agricultural, social, and economic
systems; extraordinary psychological stresses; and a
host of other difficulties is open to question. It is
clear that the ecosystem effects alone resulting from
a large-scale thermonuclear war could be enough to
destroy the current civilization in at least the Northern Hemisphere. Coupled with the direct casualties
of over 1 billion people, the combined intermediate
and long-term effects of nuclear war suggest that
eventually there might be no human survivors in the
Northern Hemisphere. Furthermore, the scenario

described here is by no means the most severe that could be imagined with present world nuclear arsenals and those contemplated for the near future. In any large-scale nuclear exchange between the superpowers, global environmental changes sufficient to cause the extinction of a major fraction of the plant and animal species on the Earth are likely. In that event, the possibility of the extinction of Homo sapiens cannot be excluded.

Sobering as these long-term possibilities may be, we need not venture beyond the immediate—and much more clearly predictable—increment in human suffering to seal our conviction that nuclear winter represents a great danger, heretofore unrecognized. The probable collapse of northern hemisphere agriculture in a crowded and hungry world is potential disaster enough.

The prospect of nuclear winter, however frightening, may at least (and at last) teach us that we are truly one world and that the result of nuclear war, for any one nation, could only be the most ultimately empty of all "victories".

RECOGNIZING AUTHOR'S POINT OF VIEW

This activity may be used as an individualized study guide for students in libraries and resource centers or as a discussion catalyst in small group and classroom discussions.

A. Many readers do not make clear distinctions between descriptive articles that relate factual information and articles that express a point of view. Articles that express editorial commentary and analysis are featured in this publication. Examine the following statements. Then try to decide if any of these statements take a similar position to any readings in chapter two. Working as individuals or in small groups, try to match the point of view in each statement below with the most appropriate reading in chapter two. Mark the **appropriate reading number** in front of each statement. Mark (0) for any statement that cannot be associated with the point of view of any opinion in chapter two.

____**Statement one:** A major nuclear war would bring about the destruction of the human race.

____**Statement two:** A nuclear winter as described in the popular press would be an unlikely event, following a major nuclear exchange.

____**Statement three:** Nuclear winter after a major nuclear exchange is practically unavoidable.

____**Statement four:** The scientific evidence thus far does not support the idea of nuclear winter in the aftermath of a major nuclear exchange by the superpowers.

____**Statement five:** During and after a nuclear winter, species extinction on a massive global scale could be expected.

____**Statement six:** Nuclear winter is unlikely to occur because the heat from burning cities will offset the cooling.

____ **Statement seven:** How could the theory of nuclear winter be correct when it has been overlooked for so many years?

____ **Statement eight:** President Reagan's star wars defense program will help prevent nuclear winter.

____ **Statement nine:** The world will always have to live with the threat of nuclear war.

____ **Statement ten:** Mutual reduction in the level of nuclear weapons is the best way to avoid nuclear war.

B. Summarize the author's point of view in one sentence for each of the readings in chapter two as indicated below.

Reading 4_____

_____

_____

Reading 5_____

_____

_____

Reading 6_____

_____

_____

Reading 7_____

_____

_____

CHAPTER 3

NUCLEAR STRATEGY
AND NUCLEAR WINTER

8   NO NEED TO CHANGE
     U.S. NUCLEAR STRATEGY
     Caspar Weinberger

9   STRATEGY CHANGES ARE MANDATORY
     Anthony E. Scoville

10   LIMITED NUCLEAR WAR STRATEGY
     MAY BE NECESSARY
     Leon Sloss

11   PLANNING NUCLEAR WAR-FIGHTING
     STRATEGIES IS INSANE
          Physicians for Social Responsibility

12   STRATEGIC DEFENSE AND NUCLEAR
     WINTER: THE POINT
     Richard Perle

13   STRATEGIC DEFENSE AND NUCLEAR
     WINTER: THE COUNTERPOINT
     Theodore A. Postol

NUCLEAR STRATEGY

NO NEED TO CHANGE U.S. NUCLEAR STRATEGY

Caspar Weinberger

Caspar W. Weinberger served as Secretary of Defense in the Reagan Administration. The following comments are excerpted from a Pentagon study of nuclear winter. This report titled, The Potential Effects of Nuclear War on the Climate, *was mandated by the Congress.*

Points to Consider

1. Why is no change in U.S. nuclear strategy necessary in light of information about nuclear winter?
2. How is the policy of "deterrence" defined?
3. What is meant by the term "strategic modernization program?"
4. What is the "strategic defense initiative" and how will it help avoid a nuclear winter?

Caspar W. Weinberger, *The Potential Effects of Nuclear War on the Climate,* March, 1985, pp. 9-15.

By preventing the detonation of thousands of nuclear warheads, the Strategic Defense Initiative may provide an answer to both the short-term and potential longer-term consequences of nuclear war.

The Department of Defense recognizes the importance of improving our understanding of the technical underpinnings of the hypothesis which asserts, in its most rudimentary form, that if sufficient material, smoke, and dust are created by nuclear explosions, lofted to sufficient altitude, and were to remain at altitude for protracted periods, deleterious effects would occur with regard to the earth's climate.

We have very little confidence in the near-term ability to predict this phenomenon quantitatively, either in terms of the amount of sunlight obscured and the related temperature changes, the period of time such consequences may persist, or of the levels of nuclear attacks which might initiate such consequences. We do not know whether the long-term consequences of a nuclear war—of whatever magnitude—would be the often postulated months of subfreezing temperatures, or a considerably less severely perturbed atmosphere. Even with widely ranging and unpredictable weather, the destructiveness for human survival of the less severe climatic effects might be of a scale similar to the other horrors associated with nuclear war. . . .

The issues raised by the possibility of effects of nuclear war on the atmosphere and climate only strengthen the basic imperative of U.S. national security policy—that nuclear war must be prevented. For over three decades, we have achieved this objective through deterrence and in the past 20 years we have sought to support it through arms control. Now, through the Strategic Defense Initiative, we are seeking a third path to reduce the threat of nuclear devastation. . . .

In this report, we will first discuss these three principal elements of our posture—deterrence, arms control, and the Strategic Defense Initiative—briefly describing each one and discussing how it relates to the issue of possible severe climatic effects. We conclude, in this regard, that these three elements, and the initiatives we are taking for each of them, remain fundamentally sound. . . .

Deterrence

The evolution of U.S. strategic doctrine from the late-1940s to date is well documented. Throughout the past four decades, our policy has had to convince the Soviet leadership of the futility of aggression by ensuring that we possessed a deterrent which was sufficiently credible and capable to respond to any potential attack. Two years ago next month, the President's Commission on Strategic Forces (Snowcroft report) confirmed anew that effective deterrence requires:

- Holding at risk those military, political and economic assets which the Soviet leadership have given every indications by their actions they value most and which constitute their tools of power and control;

- Creating a stable strategic balance by eliminating unilateral Soviet advantages and evolving to increasingly survivable deterrent forces; and

- Maintaining a modern, effective strategic Triad by strengthening each of its legs and emphasizing secure and survivable command, control and communications.

These three principles are reflected in our strategic modernization program discussed below. Consistent with meeting our essential targeting requirements which derive from these three overarching deterrence principles, we also observe other policy considerations, three of which warrant special mention because they may serve to reduce concerns about climatic effects. They are a reduction of the number of weapons and total yield, rejection of targeting urban population as a way of achieving deterrence, and escalation control. Reducing unwanted damage must be an important feature of our policy, not only because of a categorical desire to limit damage that is not necessary, but also because it adds to the credibility of our response if attacked and thus strengthens deterrence. Over the past 20 years or so, this policy and other considerations have resulted in development of systems which are more discriminating. This, in turn, has led to reductions of some 30% of the total number of weapons and nearly a factor of four reduction in the total yield of our stockpile. This direction continues today, and the prospects for extremely accurate and highly effective non-nuclear systems are encouraging. . . .

Preventing War

This author has no mandate to defend either the nuclear policy of the U.S. Government, or its current approach to the nuclear winter thesis, but he can find little in official policy that merits criticism.

Consistent with posing the kind of threats needed to maintain stability in deterrence for the prevention of war, the United States is endeavoring to field forces and develop targeting plans that would, if ever executed, inflict the least unwanted collateral damage upon targets that could provide the most potent fuel base for adverse climatic effects.

Colin S. Gray, National Institute for Public Policy, March , 1985

The United States has, or is now taking, specific actions which relate directly to maintaining and strengthening deterrence and reducing the dangers of nuclear war: the President's Strategic Modernization Program, arms reductions initiatives, and the Strategic Defense Initiative all bear directly to maintaining and strengthening deterrence and reducing the dangers of nuclear war: the President's Strategic Modernization Program, arms reductions initiatives, and the Strategic Defense Initiative all bear directly on effective deterrence, and are all therefore relevant to the potential destructiveness of nuclear war including possible climatic effects. We will now discuss these in turn.

Strategic Modernization Program

The President's Strategic Modernization Program is designed to maintain effective deterrence, and by doing so, is also an important measure in minimizing the risks of atmospheric or climatic effects. It is providing significantly enhanced command, control, communications and intelligence (C^3I) capabilities which, through their increased survivability and effectiveness contribute immeasurably to our ability to control escalation. Survivable C^3I contributes to escalation control and thus, as explained above, to mitigation of damage levels (of whatever kind, including possible climatic effects) by reducing pressures for immediate or expanded use of nuclear weapons out of fear that capability for future release would be lost. The improvements to our sea-based, bomber and land-based legs of our Triad—all intended also to improve survivability and effectiveness—are also essential to maintaining deterrence. . . .

Arms Reductions

It is the position of this Administration that the level of nuclear weapons which exists today is unacceptably high. As a result, to the extent it is possible to reduce nuclear weapons unilaterally—particularly where both conventional and nuclear modernization programs allow replacement of existing systems on a less than one-for-one basis—we have undertaken to do so. But it would be misleading to suggest that dramatic reductions in nuclear weapons can be achieved by unilateral U.S. initiatives without increasing the risk of nuclear attack, in the absence of any indication that the Soviet Union is undertaking similar steps, or short of a changed strategic situation resulting from highly effective strategic defenses.

Major reductions in nuclear weapons can only be achieved by negotiating mutual and verifiable reduction agreements. Agreements which only legitimate the growth, or slow the rate of increase, of existing stockpiles are not in our national interest. It is for this reason that the Administration has determined that SALT II is fatally flawed. Since 1981, the Reagan Administration has demonstrated its strong desire to break with the past pattern of calling buildups "arms control". The arms reduction proposals we have put forward have been the most extensive ones advanced by either side for over 20 years. . . .

The Strategic Defense Initiative and Arms Control

It is essential to keep potential benefits of arms reductions clearly in view when assessing what one seeks to accomplish through that process. Our objectives in arms reductions are to preserve deterrence in the near-term and begin a transition to a more stable world, with greatly reduced levels of nuclear arms and an enhanced ability to deter war based upon the increasing contribution of non-nuclear

A PRIMER ON MODERN DAY DEFENSE STRATEGIES:

CURRENT STRATEGY: MUTUAL ASSURED DESTRUCTION (MAD)

PROPOSED BY BLEEDING HEART LIBERALS: UNILATERAL NUCLEAR FREEZE

PROPOSED BY SO-CALLED, "DOVES:" BILATERAL VERIFIABLE NUCLEAR FREEZE

PROPOSED BY HAWKS: STRATEGIC DEFENSE INITIATIVE (STAR WARS)

ASAY COLORADO SPRINGS SUN.

defenses against offensive nuclear arms. This period of transition could lead to the eventual elimination of all nuclear arms, both offensive and defensive. A world free of nuclear arms is an ultimate objective to which we, the Soviet Union, and all other nations can agree. The Strategic Defense Iniatiative research program enhances our efforts to seek verifiable reductions in offensive weapons through arms control negotiations. Such defenses would destroy nuclear weapons before they could reach their targets, thereby multiplying the gains made through negotiated reductions. Indeed, even a single-layer defense may provide a greater mitigating effect on atmospheric consequences than could result from any level of reductions likely to be accepted by the USSR in the near term.

In addition to its design objective to destroy nuclear weapons in flight, the Strategic Defense Initiative would further serve to remove any potential for environmental disaster by moving away from the concept of deterring nuclear war by threat of retaliation and, instead, moving towards deterrence by denial of an attacker's political and military objective. . . .

Thus, by preventing the detonation of thousands of nuclear warheads, and, by paving the way for the elimination of those warheads by making them obsolete, the Strategic Defense Initiative may provide an answer to both the short-term and potential longer-term consequences of nuclear war. . . .

Civil Defense

The basic goal of civil defense in the United States is to develop and maintain a humanitarian program to save lives in the event of major emergency, including a nuclear war. As to changes in our Civil Defense posture, the Federal Emergency Management Agency believes that until scientific knowledge regarding climatic impacts of nuclear conflicts is more fully developed it would be impractical to develop cost-effective policies regarding civil defense, or to change existing policies.

The particular staff elements within the Federal Emergency Management Agency responsible for civil defense planning are being kept abreast of the issues relative to possible climate effects as they develop and will be prepared to take appropriate action as soon as the relevant research now underway is complete.

Conclusion

As we have shown, much of our long standing policy and our current initiatives move in a direction such as to reduce the probability of severe climatic effects even though they were instituted before such effects were under investigation. Specifically, we are maintaining a strong deterrence augmented by necessary force modernization and verifiable, mutual arms reductions. We are continuing the development of accurate, discriminating systems designed to achieve their military objectives with the least nuclear yield possible. We have implemented and are constantly refining options for escalation control. We have, long ago, rejected the targeting of population as a means of securing deterrence. Finally, we have begun the Strategic Defense Initiative which has as its ultimate goal the obsolescence of nuclear weapons. All these things work first to deter nuclear war—the best way of avoiding the effects at issue—and second, to reduce these effects were deterrence to fail.

STRATEGY CHANGES
ARE MANDATORY

Anthony E. Scoville

Anthony E. Scoville is a technical consultant to the House Science and Technology Committee. His scientific studies have included the greenhouse effect, nuclear winter, and the possibilities of world climate change.

Points to Consider

1. Why does the "Weinberger Report" underestimate the likelihood of nuclear winter?
2. How is the TTAPS report described?
3. How long might nuclear winter last?
4. What is meant by the term "nuclear self-deterrence and how is the concept related to nuclear winter?
5. Why does nuclear winter provide us with the alternative to dismantle all nuclear weapons?

Excerpted from testimony by Anthony E. Scoville before the House Committee on Interior and Insular Affairs, March 14, 1985.

Knowledge of the nuclear winter provides an alternative. It tells us that it is possible to dismantle all nuclear weapons with the assurance that any nation which violated the prohibition would be deterred by the assurance of suicide.

I want to express my concern over Secretary of Defense Weinberger's report to Congress, "The Potential Effects of Nuclear War on The Climate". While serving as a Technical Consultant to the House Science and Technology Committee I had the opportunity to study the Greenhouse Effect which may result from fossil energy use; more recently I have been writing a book surveying potential causes of world climate change including the "nuclear winter". Based on my experience I believe the report is a gravely inadequate response to the mandate of Section 1107 of the 1985 Department of Defense Authorization Act. The report seriously underestimates the likelihood of a nuclear winter and its implications for US arms control and defense policy.

First, while concluding that "Even with widely ranging and unpredictable weather, the destructiveness for human survival of the less severe climatic effects might be of a scale similar to the other horrors associated with nuclear war", (p.9) the report severely criticizes the seminal TTAPS study by Turco, Sagan and their colleagues because the latter is based on a one-dimensional model of the atmosphere. Nowhere does the Secretary mention the more recent work by Stephen Schneider and his colleagues using the three-dimensional atmospheric model developed at the National Center for Atmospheric Research. They conclude that "continental interiors may cool by 40°C or more in July (similar to the land values of Turco et al.) but land surfaces can cool more quickly, to below freezing—even near coasts—in only a few days. . . .(Nature 310, 626, 1984).

I should add that the strong temperature contrasts between land and the oceans suggest the likely occurrence of hurricane strength storms along coasts where human populations are concentrated.

75

Second, even the report's conclusion that "severe climatic effects might be of a scale similar to the other horrors associated with nuclear war" is flawed in part because the report ignores the "environmental and biological consequences". Conventional analyses of the casualties resulting from a major nuclear exchange between the US and the USSR range from a low of 200 megadeaths worldwide up to two billion dead resulting from the combined effects of fire, blast, and radiation. Unprecedented though such losses would be, approximately two to three billion people were expected by these analyses to survive a nuclear holocaust. The "nuclear winter" with its attendant subfreezing temperatures and crop failures even in tropical regions threatens mass starvation the world over. In the words of the panel of biologists at the Conference on the Long-Term Worldwide Biological Consequences of Nuclear War: "In any large scale nuclear exchange between the superpowers, global environmental changes sufficient to cause the extinction of a major fraction of the plant and animal species of the Earth are likely. In that event, the possibility of the extinction of Homo sapiens cannot be excluded." (Science, Vol. 222, p. 1300)

The report is further flawed when it suggests that these environmental and biological consequences of "newly postulated climatic effects" would only occur "at possible upper extremes indicated by some analyses" (p.ii). The TTAPS report was startling precisely because it concluded that a nuclear winter could occur if less than 1% (100 megatons) of world strategic nuclear arsenals were detonated over urban targets.

Since the TTAPS report was published evidence has come forward that the effects of a nuclear winter would be prolonged up to four years after a nuclear exchange because increased snow and sea ice particularly in high latitudes would reflect more summer sunlight than normal. As stated by Alan Robock of the Univ. of Maryland Dept. of Meteorology, "the response of the climate to nuclear war is longer and larger than previously found by Turco et al. (TTAPS) who did not include these (snow-ice) feedbacks. It would presumably be very difficult to grow crops not only in the summer of the year that the war began, but also in the summer of the next year, with temperatures over land almost 6°C (10°F) colder than normal." (Nature, 310, p.668)

During this period of prolonged cold stretching over several years, the viability of seeds would sharply diminish reducing the germination of crops even were young plants not hampered by cold.

In sum, Secretary Weinberger's report does not provide an adequate review of current technical knowledge of the climatic and environmental effects of a "nuclear winter".

Nuclear Self-Deterrence

More serious, however, is the failure of the report to address the policy implications of a nuclear winter. Instead, the report takes the position that possible climate change after nuclear war merely supports current nuclear policies. Thus it states, "We conclude. . .that these three elements (deterrence, arms control, and the Strategic Defense Initiative) and the initiatives we are taking for each of them, remain fundamentally sound." (p.10). The report does not seriously consider the fact that the nuclear winter introduces a new concept of deterrence: namely, self-deterrence. "Nuclear Self-Deterrence", nuclear aggression can be deterred by the knowledge that any nation who launched a nuclear first strike of sufficient size to incapacitate either superpower would experience starvation of its entire population even if the target nation never launched a single missile in retaliation. Thus nuclear self-deterrence opens up the possibility of dramatic unilateral reductions in nuclear arms as an indication of good will leading to the negotiated elimination of all nuclear weapons.

Secretary Weinberger criticizes "self-deterrence" because of the alleged scientific uncertainties of climate models and because the Soviets would not find self-deterrence credible given these "uncertainties". I have already discussed the technical inaccuracies in his analysis of our scientific understanding of climate after nuclear war. Furthermore, Soviet scientists, high-level academicians, not mere "propagandists" as the Secretary suggests, have spoken out forcefully on the threat of the nuclear winter. That Soviet leaders may recognize the threat as well is demonstrated by the participation of these scientists in the live television conference which occurred as part of the October, 1983 Conference on The World After Nuclear War. Such participation would surely not have occurred without political permission from the highest level.

Implicitly the Secretary also dismisses nuclear self-deterrence with the assertion: "We believe that threatening civilian populations is neither a prudent nor a moral means of achieving deterrence, . . .our strategy consciously does not target population and, in fact, has provisions for reducing civilian casualties."(p.11).

Nowhere in his report does the Secretary explain how one might prevent the mere 100 megatons required to initiate a nuclear winter from striking populated areas when so many military targets in the Soviet Union and Europe are located in or near urban areas. Rather, he seems to draw a conclusion precisely opposite to self-deterrence when the report says: "that proposals which would 'freeze development of modernized systems would also stop what has been a continuing trend in our capability—development of systems which are more discriminating and thus more restrictive in both local and global effects. We must avoid constraints that would force us to use weapons of high yield or unconfined effects." (p.13).

Rationale for Nuclear Build-up

This statement comes close to using the nuclear winter as a rationale for developing a nuclear war fighting capability—an extraordinarily ominous signal which must surely be perceived as a deadly threat by Soviet leaders.

Similarly, the Secretary argues that the Strategic Defense Initiative (Star Wars) "may provide a greater mitigating effect on atmospheric consequences than could result from any level of reductions likely to be accepted by the USSR in the

Aftermath of a Nuclear Winter

near term." (p.13) It is incomprehensible how the Secretary believes that it will be possible to develop the enormously complex and error prone computer programs required to command and control a space-based missile defense system when he so seriously doubts the relatively simple computer models of the atmosphere which predict the occurrence of a nuclear winter.

President Reagan is correct when he seeks some alternative to the balance of terror which has been the basis of nuclear deterrence for the last forty years. Sooner or later that delicate balance will be upset with catastrophic consequences for mankind. But he is dangerously deluded when he concludes that there is a technical fix to the political problem resolving superpower conflicts. There is no technical fix, whether in the guise of conventional "mutual assured destruction" or a microchip moat of strategic missile defenses, which will work perfectly, forever—as it must—now that mankind knows the secret of nuclear energy.

An Alternative

Knowledge of the nuclear winter provides an alternative. It tells us that it is possible to dismantle all nuclear weapons with the assurance that any nation which violated the prohibition would be deterred by the assurance of suicide.

Secretary Weinberger's report on the climatic effects of nuclear war is alarming. It suggests that our vision of superpower defense and foreign policy is so astigmatized by pre-nuclear categories of deterrence and counterdeterrence that intelligent men can seriously employ the nuclear winter to rationalize an acceleration of the strategic arms race which has emperiled mankind for forty years. It suggests that mankind may not negotiate a path to the post-nuclear era—in time.

10   NUCLEAR STRATEGY

LIMITED NUCLEAR WAR STRATEGY MAY BE NECESSARY

Leon Sloss

Leon Sloss is the president of Leon Sloss Associates, Inc. His consulting firm has studied the major technical reports on nuclear winter as they apply to strategic nuclear policy issues.

Points to Consider

1. How and why have studies exaggerated nuclear war scenarios?
2. What different nuclear war scenarios are possible?
3. Why is a limited nuclear war possible?
4. Why is it necessary to have limited nuclear war fighting strategies?

Excerpted from testimony by Leon Sloss before the Senate Armed Services Committee, October 2 and 3, 1985.

I think a limited nuclear war is possible because all parties involved will have a very strong interest in keeping it limited.

I appreciate the opportunity to appear once again before this committee on a matter of importance to our national security. I am not here as an expert on the technical aspects of nuclear winter, although I have examined the major studies that have been undertaken by technical experts and I have a general understanding of the scientific phenomena insofar as we know them. Instead, I will focus my remarks on policy issues, with particular emphasis on nuclear strategy, targeting policy and weapons development.

First, I would like to say a few words about the importance of the nuclear winter issue because I think it has been both exaggerated and understated in public discussion. There is a great deal we do not yet know about the phenomenology associated with very large fires and firestorms and the resultant effects on the global environment. Yet, I believe that we know enough to take the issue of nuclear winter seriously. At the same time, I am concerned that some of the most widely publicized studies and statements on the subject have tended to exaggerate the problem by basing their analyses on unrepresentative scenarios of nuclear war.

Nuclear War Scenarios

Let me begin then by discussing scenarios. It is certainly possible to imagine nuclear wars in which there are large or massive attacks on cities, but in these scenarios the nuclear winter phenomena is likely to be inconsequential in relation to the direct effects (e.g., blast) and fallout. In my view, the scenarios on which we ought to concentrate our attention are those in which the attack focuses on military targets (some of which may indeed be in cities). These are cases where there could still be substantial worldwide climatic effects which would extend well beyond and possibly magnify the direct effects. For example, attacks on military targets in wooded areas could create large fires. We do not yet know very much about these effects, in part because most of the studies to date have assumed very large attacks on cities.

However, the impact on the global climate apparently would be less than in large attacks on cities; but it may still be substantial enough to concern us.

In postulating nuclear winter scenarios we must invariably make some basic assumptions about national defense strategy and the role of nuclear weapons in that strategy. Needless-to-say, analysts often hold different beliefs and assumptions. Some will argue that a limited nuclear war in which cities are avoided or largely avoided is unrealistic; that once any nuclear weapons are used escalation to a very large scale nuclear war would be automatic. I do not agree, but if this were true we could stop worrying about nuclear winter. As I have already suggested, the direct effects would overwhelm the climatic effects. (Perhaps we should worry nevertheless about the effects on the climate of the Southern Hemisphere, but this is quite another matter and one on which there is very little solid data so far.)

Limited Nuclear War

I think a limited nuclear war is possible because all parties involved will have a very strong interest in keeping it limited. They may find it impossible to do so; I shall address that question below. The United States has certainly made plans to limit use of nuclear weapons and to control escalation. We have reason to believe that the Soviet Union, while expressing public skepticism about limiting nuclear war, has capabilities and plans which would permit them to do so.

Some observers also argue that planning to limit a nuclear war is dangerous because it leads to acceptance of the possibility of such a war. The possibility does exist, however remote, but it seems to me far worse to have no plans to control escalation or terminate a conflict before it becomes a total holocaust. I would be deeply disturbed and angry if my government did not have such plans. This does not mean that I am confident such plans will work. But it seems to me to be beyond argument that we are better off having such plans than having no options save surrender or all-out war. More important, every President and Secretary of Defense who has had to live with the responsibility for nuclear weapons seems to have arrived at the same conclusion.

If we are to concentrate on limited nuclear war scenarios and on climatological outcomes in which the decline in temperature is less pronounced and less prolonged than in the extreme cases, then it is appropriate to ask whether our plans and our weapons systems have adequately taken into account these phenomena. Unfortunately, I cannot go into nuclear plans in any detail in this forum, nor am I the appropriate person to do so. However, I would point out that U.S. planners have had to be concerned for some time (long before nuclear winter became a prominent issue) with so-called collateral effects, that is unintended damage to targets that were not the objective of a particular attack. That damage might be direct (e.g., from blast) or indirect (e.g., from fallout). Plans have been made and weapons have been designed for many years to minimize these effects, including the possibility of withholding attacks in certain instances. Now I want to be clear that it is not possible to conduct a war (with nuclear or nonnuclear weapons) without creating unintended damage. Wars are just too destructive and too unpredictable to expect that. But it is possible to minimize such unintended damage, and that can make a very substantial difference.

Minimizing Damage

One way that we have tried to do that over the years is by making our nuclear weapons smaller and more accurate. In the future it may be possible to make nonnuclear weapons that can do some of the jobs now done by nuclear weapons, and I believe it is important that we press ahead to try to do

that, although I do not believe that we can ever hope to substitute fully nonnuclear for nuclear weapons simply by pressing technology. Thus, we ought also to continue development of nuclear weapons that create less unwanted damage. There are some possibilities here as well, in addition to continued improvements in accuracy, which should enable us to make weapons smaller. For example, one development is the earth-penetrating weapon, which can create substantial ground shock but little or no atmospheric effects. I think that weapon ought to receive more attention than it has, given the current concern with nuclear winter.

I have said that our plans do seek to minimize collateral damage as a result of the way that we target weapons. It would seem prudent, as we learn more about the effects of nuclear winter, that the appropriate authorities reexamine those plans, and adjust them if that is necessary, to take account of these effects.

Some commentators have suggested that the best way to assure that we never have nuclear winter is to reduce the levels of nuclear weapons below the threshold at which such effects could occur. I consider such an approach to be impractical. First, we do not know where that threshold lies today and are unlikely to know with any confidence for years if ever. Second, unless we are to reduce our weapons inventories unilaterally (a course of action which most arms control experts, myself included, would reject as dangerous and ineffective) we are talking about undertaking a diplomatic task that has defied our best efforts at negotiation for more than two decades. I am not suggesting that negotiated reductions are impossible or that we should abandon efforts to achieve such reductions, but given the past record, I do maintain that we need to consider other alternatives. I believe these lie in continuing our past efforts to make our weapons more discriminate and our plans more flexible. Not only will this reduce the prospects of a nuclear winter should nuclear weapons ever be used, it also is the best way to strengthen deterrence, for a force whose use is plausible is a far better deterrent than one whose use would be suicidal.

In sum, my conclusions are as follows:

Phenomena associated with "Nuclear winter" constitute potential collateral effects that should be examined seriously.

More attention should be given to the worldwide climatic effects of more limited attacks and "mild" nuclear winter.

There are things we can do, if this appears necessary, to minimize nuclear winter effects through the design of weapons and the adjustment of war plans.

NUCLEAR STRATEGY

PLANNING NUCLEAR WAR-FIGHTING STRATEGIES IS INSANE

Physicians for Social Responsibility

Physicians for Social Responsibility (PSR) is a national, non-profit organization of physicians, dentists and medical students dedicated to professional and public education on the medical hazards of nuclear weapons and nuclear war.

PSR was formed in 1961 by a group of physicians who were troubled by the health implications of nuclear weapons testing in the atmosphere and the lack of data on the medical consequences of nuclear war. The organization played a major role in developing public understanding of the devastating capabilities of thermonuclear weapons, which contributed to the realization of the Limited Test Ban Treaty in 1963. In 1979, concerned about the hazards of nuclear weapons proliferation, physicians reactivated the dormant organization.

Points to Consider

1. What do U.S. policy makers say about nuclear war-fighting strategy?
2. How is a full-scale nuclear war described?
3. What is meant by the term, "the final epidemic?"

Excerpted from a public position paper by the Physicians for Social Responsibility on nuclear war-fighting strategies, 1985.

"Everybody's going to make it if there are enough shovels to go around. . .Dig a hole, cover it with a couple of doors and then throw three feet of dirt on top. It's the dirt that does it."

T.K. Jones
Deputy Undersecretary of Defense for Strategic and Theater Nuclear Forces

Nuclear-Attack Plans

How does one respond to such madness? Do our policymakers understand the consequences of the policies they propose? We think not.

Millions of Americans fear an all-out nuclear war within the next ten years, with understandable cause.

Some future trouble spot in the Caribbean, Middle East or elsewhere could well become the catalyst. If nothing else, the Soviet Union's downing of an unarmed passenger plane demonstrates how easily an itchy trigger finger, an error of judgment or a mechanical malfunction could cause a nuclear debacle in which millions, rather than hundreds, of lives would be massacred.

Nuclear War-Fighting

In spite of the recent and welcomed agreement to hold nuclear arms talks, our own policymakers in Washington continue to pursue a nuclear "war-fighting" capability. In order to deter nuclear war, they now argue, we must be prepared to win a nuclear war with the Soviet Union. This optimism is based on the hollow premise that American society can, in any meaningful sense, survive the ultimate holocaust.

In the Pentagon's Five-Year Plan, Secretary of Defense Weinberger states that U.S. forces must be capable of "controlled nuclear counterattacks over a protracted period. . ." in order to "prevail and be able to force the Soviet Union to seek earliest termination of hostilities on terms favorable to the United States."

Eugene Rostow, President Reagan's first Director of the Arms Control and Disarmament Agency, sees recovery from nuclear war as a manageable problem. He has said: "Japan, after all, not only survived but flourished after a nuclear at-tack. . .Depending on certain assumptions, some estimates predict 10 million (dead) on one side and 100 million on the other. But that is not the whole population."

Mr. Rostow ignores the fact that Hiroshima was not a nuclear exchange. Only one power possessed atomic weapons. Now at least six nations possess them. The Hiroshima bomb was a fifteen kiloton device. Strategic warheads today can exceed twenty megatons. Then there was an outside world which could restore and rebuild Japan. In a future exchange, there would be no such ability to rescue the "survivors."

Full-Scale Nuclear War

In a full-scale nuclear war with the Soviet Union 100 million. . .150 million. . .or more Americans would die. More destructive power than in all of World War II would be unleashed each second during the brief hours it would take for the missiles to fall.

More people would be killed in the first few hours than in all the wars of history put together. These would be the im-mediate casualties. Those who escaped the blast would die more slowly from radiation exposure, disease, and starva-tion.

This is the bleak, unchanging reality. As physicians who have studied the medical consequences of nuclear war, we know there would be no victor—only the dead and the dying.

Because the Reagan Administration is now committed to the biggest arms buildup in our history, we of Physicians for

89

Social Responsibility are compelled to issue this grim warning based on medical and scientific analysis:

1. Nuclear war, even a "limited" one, would result in death, injury, and disease on a scale that has no precedent in the history of human existence.

2. Medical "disaster planning" for nuclear war is meaningless. There is no possible effective medical response. Most hospitals would be destroyed, most medical personnel dead or injured, most supplies unavailable. The vast majority of the "survivors" would die.

3. There is no effective civil defense against nuclear war. The blast, thermal and radiation effects would kill even those in shelters, and the fallout would reach those who had been evacuated.

4. Recovery from nuclear war would be impossible. The economic, environmental and social fabric on which human life depends would be destroyed in the U.S., the U.S.S.R., and much of the rest of the world.

5. There can be no winners in a nuclear war. Worldwide fallout would contaminate much of the globe for generations and atmospheric effects would severely damage all living things, as well as food and water supplies.

6. In sum, there is no cure for nuclear war, only prevention.

Yet, in the next five years the Administration wants to spend more than $290 billion preparing to fight a nuclear war. This policy can only accelerate the already threatening arms spiral. It will make nuclear war more likely.

The Final Epidemic

Ending the nuclear arms race is our most urgent task. Physicians for Social Responsibility (PSR) advocates a verifiable bilateral freeze on the testing, production and deployment of nuclear arms by both the United States and the Soviet Union.

We at PSR have already affected the way in which Americans and Soviets think about nuclear war. Through a series of symposia on "The Medical Consequences of Nuclear Weapons and Nuclear War" held across the country, we have spurred thousands to action. The participation of prominent leaders such as former Secretary of State Cyrus Vance, Dr. Jonas Salk and Dr. Carl Sagan has given our work

Reprinted with permission of the *Minneapolis Star and Tribune.*

national attention. We have similarly traveled to the Soviet Union and lectured extensively on the consequences of nuclear war.

From its start in 1961, PSR has recognized that a nuclear war would be the final epidemic, and we have worked to reach our fellow physicians and through them the American people with that message. Through our work, Americans have begun to question the sanity of the arms race. Eighty-nine percent of all Americans now believe that there can be no winner in a nuclear war.

In Washington and across the nation, we have spoken clearly and forcefully of the medical consequences of nuclear war and the futility of civil defense. Regardless of who is President, Congress has a critical role to play in controlling the arms race—one which PSR has long recognized. We have testified before Congressional committees and worked directly with House and Senate members and their staffs.

Because of our efforts and those of others, the House has voted to support a bilateral, verifiable nuclear weapons freeze. The Senate has called for a resumption of negotiations for a Comprehensive Test Ban Treaty. The House has voted for a moratorium on anti-satellite weapon testing. Both Houses of Congress have significantly cut back the MX missile program and resisted Presidential requests for massive increases in civil defense spending.

We have willingly taken on the challenge presented to us by governments, including our own, which refuse to acknowledge that a nuclear war is not and never will be survivable, let alone winnable. But we must work to sustain this momentum and to educate still more Americans to accept responsibility for their own survival.

Time is short. Our future rests on what we and our leaders do about nuclear policy in the days and weeks ahead.

NUCLEAR STRATEGY

STRATEGIC DEFENSE AND NUCLEAR WINTER: THE POINT

Richard Perle

Richard N. Perle is the assistant Secretary of Defense for International security Policy. He has been a key advisor for strategic nuclear policy in the Reagan Administration.

Points to Consider

1. What uncertainty exists with regard to nuclear winter?
2. What is the relationship between nuclear winter and the U.S. deterrent force?
3. What is the strategic defense initiative and what relationship does it have to nuclear winter?
4. What have the Soviets done about nuclear winter?

Excerpted from testimony by Richard N. Perle before the House Committee on Science and Technology, March 14, 1985.

The Department of Defense has understood for a very long time the immense tragedy a nuclear war would bring to the world—with or without a nuclear winter.

This administration accepts the proposition that there are levels of nuclear weapons exchange at which the phenomena described in the nuclear winter studies would occur with devastating consequences. But we recognize, and would hope that others would recognize, that there is a significant range of uncertainty as to precisely how many weapons under precisely what circumstances would produce precisely what climatic changes. We think it's important to continue to do work in order to refine those estimates and those judgments, but the range of uncertainty is very sizable indeed. And it does not, in my judgment, advance our scientific understanding when loose statements are made that attribute a degree of certainty we do not have the privilege of now possessing, to the levels at which different climatic effects would occur. When Dr. Sagan says, as he has in the past, that 100 weapons on 100 cities would be enough to produce nuclear winter, that suggests a degree of certitude that he cannot possess, because we, the scientific community, do not possess it.

We have a Research Program aimed at refining the judgments that go into understanding the phenomena involved. It's a sensible Research Program. I think there was regret expressed this morning that we had put $2.5 million rather than the $5 million recommended into it. I think there's a misunderstanding there. The total government funding is on the order of $5 million. The Defense Department contribution is roughly half of that to a broader administration effort.

Now what are the implications, granting that there is some level of nuclear exchange at which the phenomena described as nuclear winter would occur, for American policy, for our security, for world peace, for our survival, and not least of all for our freedom and independence?

The first implication that we would draw is that we had better assure the effectiveness of our deterrent force because, whether we like it or not, the best hope we have of preventing nuclear winter, and the other consequences short of nuclear winter that would nevertheless be devastating beyond belief, is to deter that war from ever taking place. And the policy of this administration and previous administrations is aimed at doing precisely that. And the programs of this administration are not different in significant respects from the programs of previous administrations. Virtually the whole of the Reagan Strategic Modernization Program, for example, has its roots in the plans and programs of previous administrations. So, first, we need to assure the effectiveness of our deterrent forces. . . .

Absent until now has been any recognition that the Department of Defense, which has been chastised for not discovering nuclear winter and for not embracing it with the same grandiose rhetoric as the administration's critics, the Department of Defense has understood for a very long time what an immense tragedy a nuclear war would be with or without nuclear winter. The idea that our policy should be fundamentally different because, instead of the destruction of hundreds of millions of people through prompt and immediate effects of a nuclear war, that our policy should be fundamentally different because we now realize that the consequences are even worse than was realized before, misses the fundamental point. We are serious about avoiding a nuclear war because the consequences that we have known about before the discovery of nuclear winter are persuasive enough reasons for avoiding a nuclear war by any means that men of good will can devise to do that. . . .

Strategic Defense

Now let me talk about the strategic defense initiative. What this administration has proposed to do is conduct a 5-year program of experimentation to find out whether the development of technologies largely in the civilian sector that could bear on the development of a strategic defense have put the United States in a position where we might be able to develop a reliable system of strategic defenses. We don't know whether it's going to prove possible or not. We know the Soviet Union is working hard on the development of such a system, has been doing so for years with increasing vigor following the ABM Treaty of 1972, and I think we ought to be smart enough to know that if we abandon our program in a manner that couldn't possibly be verified by arms control, the Soviets will carry on with their program just as they have carried on with a number of programs in violation of the existing treaties between us. . . .

I think the only sensible reaction to the situation in which we find ourselves, with massively growing Soviet offensive nuclear forces, with no certainty that we will achieve an arms control agreement that provides for significant reductions, and with a significant Soviet SDI research program on the way, is to conduct an SDI research program of our own. And if we should prove to be successful, would we not prefer that that strategic defense intercept the warheads that would produce the nuclear winter if they detonated on the surface of the earth?

I hope in particular that we can focus our time on why it should be assumed that the phenomenon of nuclear winter automatically requires that the administration change the strategic doctrine and policy of the United States, because I say to you that our policy and doctrine is aimed at preventing a nuclear war, and the potential of a nuclear winter is an even more powerful reason for preventing a nuclear war. And it is by no means obvious to me, as it evidently was to Dr. Sagan, that the discovery of nuclear winter obviously entails changes in our strategic policy. . . .

Current Policy

There is an initiative, strategic defense, which complements arms reduction and which could act, if eventually

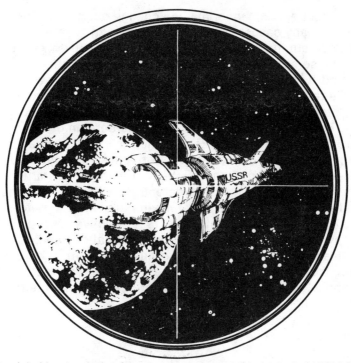

Reprinted by permission from *Imprimis,* the monthly journal of Hillsdale College, featuring presentations at Hillsdale's Center for Constructive Alternatives and at its Shavano Institute for National Leadership.

developed and deployed, to reduce the risks of war. Should deterrence fail, defenses could mitigate substantially both the short- and long-term effects by reducing the number of ballistic missile warheads that would reach their targets. This could facilitate the transition to a more stable world, with greatly reduced levels of nuclear arms and an enhanced ability to deter war based upon an increasing contribution of non-nuclear defenses. And this period of transition could lead to the eventual elimination of all nuclear arms, both offensive and defensive.

The department of defense has understood for a very long time the immense tragedy a nuclear war would bring to the world—with or without a nuclear winter. Thus, our current policies offer the prudent approach in dealing with the question of nuclear war, including its potential effect on the climate. What I find difficult to understand, therefore, is why many individuals now assume that the possibility of nuclear winter requires, demands, that we change our policy. They do so, in many cases, without even bothering to take the time to determine what our policy is, and how it works. For example, some analyses of the "nuclear winter" effect have assumed targeting of cities. If this were regarded as an inevitable result of nuclear attack, or as U.S. policy, it would completely distort analysis of climatic effects. More importantly, it would perpetuate a basic misperception of the nature of deterrence. Attacks designed to strike populations would, by virtue of deliberately targeting heavily built up urban centers, necessarily have a high probability of starting major fires. We believe that threatening civilian populations is neither a prudent nor a moral means of achieving deterrence, nor in light of Soviet views, is it effective. Our strategy intentionally does not target populations and, in fact, has provisions for reducing civilian casualties. As part of our modernization program, we are retiring older deterrent systems which might create a greater risk of climatic effect than their replacements.

NUCLEAR STRATEGY

STRATEGIC DEFENSE AND NUCLEAR WINTER: THE COUNTERPOINT

Theodore A. Postol

Theodore A. Postol made the following remarks in his capacity as a representative of the Center for International Security and Arms Control.

Points to Consider

1. What was the U.S. response to the construction of the Moscow ABM system?
2. What would happen if nations built nuclear defenses?
3. Why would a nuclear defense that protected cities be difficult to construct?
4. How could defensive weapons become dangerous offensive weapons?
5. Why might space based defensive weapons become a serious threat?

Excerpted from testimony by Theodore A. Postol before the House Subcommittee on Natural Resources, Agricultural Research, and Environment, September 12, 1984.

The consequences of defensive deployments abound with issues that could threaten to destabilize existing deterrent relationships between adversaries.

Since the question of whether or not the United States should develop and/or deploy a "Star Wars" defense has been raised in this hearing by both questions posed to me, and comments made by Dr. Teller, I would like to suggest a policy structure which each member of Congress can use as a basis for evaluating various "Star Wars" related claims and proposals.

I would recommend that the Congress support no decision to deploy or develop "Star Wars" defenses, or any other types of defenses against nuclear weapons, without first having the answers to the following five technical questions:

1. Is the defense feasible?
2. Does its application provide useful levels of protection?
3. Can it be countered?
4. Will the counters be of such a nature that the overall security posture of the country will be degraded?
5. Do the technical characteristics of the defense create new security issues?

For example, although the Soviets may have brought some very modest level of local protection with the Moscow ABM system, their defense stimulated a vast increase in the number of U.S. warheads as a counter (the U.S. MIRVed in response to the Moscow defense). The counter stimulated by the Moscow defense therefore degraded the overall security circumstance of the Soviet Union. Thus, had Soviet leadership obtained an accurate answer to question four, they might not have chosen to deploy the GALOSH system.

Consider another example. If the Soviets and the U.S. chose to build very capable defenses that only worked at low altitudes in the atmosphere, the defenses might unambiguously serve only the purpose of defense. If both sides instead built space based defenses, capable of engaging boosters at very long range, then each defense might be able to attack the other, or each defense might be used to attack the other's early warning and communications satellites. Thus, an accurate answer to question five would reveal to the Congress that the characteristics of this second type of defense would result in the introduction of a whole new set of national security problems.

Thus, the failure to obtain accurate answers to the above five technical questions could result in a costly trade of one set of national security problems for another; or worse yet, it could result in the substitution of a far more serious set of national security problems for those that certain proponents of defense have argued would be solved.

Levels of Performance

It is extremely important for members of Congress to understand that the levels of performance required of a defense will vary drastically with its mission. If the objective of the defense is to guarantee that some fraction of otherwise vulnerable nuclear forces can survive attack, guaranteeing an ability to retaliate, then much less than "perfect" defense will be adequate. If the mission of the defense is instead to guarantee the survival of a city, then the defense must be able to handle the severest and most determined of attacks with perfection. Hence, a defense that is most robust in the role of defense of nuclear forces, could be completely inadequate for defense of cities.

Although there are many roles that have been argued for a defense these two most basic ones, defense of population, and/or defense of nuclear forces are of greatest significance. If such defenses were successfully implemented by all nuclear-armed adversaries, they would drastically impact the deterrent relationship between them.

Just to illustrate how fundamental these defensive roles can be, consider the possibilty that all parties successfully implement some form of defense. If all parties successfully implemented population defenses, it would eliminate the mutual hostage relationship, an elemental characteristic of deterrence. If all parties successfully implemented a defense of otherwise vulnerable nuclear forces, it would remove any hope, and therefore any incentive, that either adversary could preemptively destroy the retaliatory capability of the other. Thus, in both possible applications, the successful implementation of complex and robust defenses by all nuclear-

Extending Nuclear Arms to Space

The U.S. government and its closest allies are out to speed up the arms drive, to extend it to space through the Star Wars program and upset the military-strategic balance.

We are calling for an end to this policy which is endangering the existence of mankind.

Eric Honecker, German Democratic Republic, May 29, 1986

armed adversaries would either enhance deterrence or eliminate the need for it.

However, if all sides depended on such defenses, powerful incentives would exist to modify or build additional forces to overwhelm them. In addition, many military planning complexities, and the ambiguities that accompany such planning, would add further complexity to an already complex structure of interacting military and political incentives.

For example, a situation could arise where two adversaries choose to defend vulnerable nuclear forces. One builds a very capable defense for only part of its force, the other builds a modest defense for all of its force.

In this postulated circumstance, the adversary with the partially defended nuclear force might then have a strong incentive to use its undefended force to destroy as much of its enemy's defended force as the offense-defense interaction would allow. Then if its enemy responded by retaliating, the remainder of its nuclear force might then be defendable, resulting in a post-exchange superiority of the attacker. If the attacker's defenses were sufficiently flexible, they might even be used to try and limit damage to cities as well as retaliatory forces.

Complicating Problems

While it by no means follows that such a situation would evolve from deterrent postures based on defended nuclear

102

forces, complications would abound, and technical intricacies of force disposition and system capabilities could potentially be of considerable military significance. For these reasons, it cannot be accepted at face value that the successful implementation of defenses for nuclear forces or population results in enhanced deterrence.

Further complicating the problem is that each adversary might simply build more warheads to attack each others cities and nuclear forces. Warheads could be reallocated so as to stress or destroy certain critical components of defenses. Tactics could be modified, sensors could be attacked, sabotage might be attempted, and devices to confuse or exhaust the defense could be built. Neither side might have confidence that they could successfully retaliate if attacked, and neither side might have confidence that their defense was in fact working.

In reality, a defense deployed to defend nuclear forces would have a finite capability. Whether or not it is, by some measure, very capable or very limited, it would only be able to intercept a finite number of attacking warheads. If enough warheads arrived in a sufficiently short interval of time, it might be overwhelmed. In addition, even with very advanced and capable sensors, it might not be able to tell decoys from real warheads. Even a very robust and capable defense would have such limits, and the viability of the defense would depend on the scale, innovation, and determination of any enemy attack against it.

If instead the defense was deployed to protect cities, only the smallest amount of success would be required of the offense, and only perfect performance could be tolerated of the defense. Thus, any meaningful level of city defense would demand a most commanding superiority of defense over offense. While it is not provable that such a combination of unchallengable superiority and perfection in performance could never be achieved, it would be unprecedented in the history of human conflict.

Defensive Characteristics

I would now like to briefly expand on the issue of defense characteristics, raised by my proposed fifth question. As I have already noted, defenses of apparently equal capability, but different characteristics, could have a very different af-

"Sure, I know what I wanna' be when I grow up. Man I just wanna be alive."

fect on the deterrent relationship between adversaries.

If, for example, two adversaries could build "perfect" defenses, utilizing some as yet unknown principle of physics to build a force field which no nuclear weapons could penetrate, then the mutual hostage relationship which is so elemental to deterrence would cease to exist. However, it would also cease to be important as a means of avoiding the catastrophe of a nuclear war.

But what if the defense was not a shield, but instead was a very powerful, very long range and irresistably potent beam of energy, capable of knocking anything out of the sky, anywhere around the earth. Could not two such enormously potent systems also attack each other?

If both adversaries possessed two such perfect defenses, then a clear and unambiguous advantage would accompany the adversary that struck first. First negating the enemy's defense, then threatening the enemy with a nuclear attack which could no longer be deterred by threats of retaliation.

Spaced Based Defenses

Nowhere is this question of defense characteristics more worrisome than when the defenses are based in space. One can imagine large and capable battle stations, that if sufficiently capable to engage ballistic missiles, would surely be able to engage each other. In fact, if they could not, the defense would not be capable of its most important function, defending itself so that it can survive to defend its masters!

However, what if one adversary chose to defend itself with a space based system, while the other instead chose a ground based one. Since many (but by no means all) ground based defense concepts have the capability to attack incoming ballistic warheads while they are still in space (at altitudes of hundreds of miles), they might also be capable of attacking space based battle stations, which would likely be at no higher altitudes than incoming warheads, and move at no higher speeds. Since the ground based system would not have to be lifted into space, it could be hardened to a space based counterattack much more easily than the orbiting system. In this circumstance, the differing characteristics of the defenses would result in an unambiguous assymmetry, leaving one side exposed to the unanswerable threats of the other.

Thus, the consequences of defensive deployments abound with issues that could threaten to destabilize existing deterrent relationships between adversaries. For this reason, a decision to deploy defenses against nuclear weapons, without first answering the five basic technical questions posed above, would in my view be highly imprudent.

INTERPRETING EDITORIAL CARTOONS

This activity may be used as an individualized study guide for students in libraries and resource centers or as a discussion catalyst in small group and classroom discussions.

Although cartoons are usually humorous, the main intent of most political cartoonists is not to entertain. Cartoons express serious social comment about important issues. Using graphic and visual arts, the cartoonist expresses opinions and attitudes. By employing an entertaining and often light-hearted visual format, cartoonists may have as much or more impact on national and world issues as editorial and syndicated columnists.

Points to Consider

1. Examine the two cartoons in this activity.

2. How would you describe the message of each cartoon? Try to describe each message in one to three sentences.

3. Do you agree with the message expressed in either cartoon? Why or why not?

4. Do either of the cartoons support the author's point of view in any of the readings in this book? If the answer is yes, be specific about which reading or readings and why.

5. Are any of the readings in chapter three in basic agreement with either of the cartoons?

"This is the moral way!"

CHAPTER 4

PREVENTING A NUCLEAR HOLOCAUST

14 A NUCLEAR WAR IS IMPROBABLE
    Fred Schwarz

15 WE ARE CLOSE TO EXTINCTION
        Union of Concerned Scientists

16 CIVIL DEFENSE AND SURVIVAL:
    THE POINT
        Leon Goure

17 CIVIL DEFENSE AND SURVIVAL:
    THE COUNTERPOINT
        Leon Baya

PREVENTING A NUCLEAR HOLOCAUST

A NUCLEAR WAR
IS IMPROBABLE

Fred Schwarz

Fred Schwarz is the author and publisher of a newsletter called the Christian Anti-Communism Crusade.

Points to Consider

1. How are Soviet leaders described?
2. What is their attitude toward nuclear winter?
3. What is the role of nuclear weapons?
4. Why is nuclear war improbable?

Dr. Fred Schwarz, "How Probable is Nuclear War?" *Christian Anti-Communism Crusade,* January 15, 1986, pp. 1-3.

A major nuclear war in which the Soviet Union and the United States fire their nuclear arsenals is likewise possible, but its probability is comparable to that of the destruction of the earth by a meteoric collision.

There are many major worldwide disasters which "might" happen but which most sensible people ignore when making plans for the future. Consider someone selecting land on which to build a home. There are many things to consider such as the firmness of the foundation, the likelihood of flooding, the probability of brushfires, and the quality of the neighborhood. But one thing that would receive little, if any, consideration is the possibility that the area would be devastated by the impact of a large meteor from outer space, even though such an eventuality is possible.

A major nuclear war in which the Soviet Union and the United States fire their nuclear arsenals is likewise possible, but its probability is comparable to that of the destruction of the earth by a meteoric collison.

There are three reasons why a major nuclear war is extremely improbable:

1. *Nuclear Winter:*

The rulers of the Soviet Union are not suicidal. Their objective is the conquest and control of the world, not the destruction of themselves and the entire Russian people. If they fired their nuclear weapons for any reason whatever, there is the distinct possibility that they would destroy both the Russian people and themselves.

Soviet literature warns frequently about the creation of a "nuclear winter" if the nuclear weapons in the arsenals of the U.S.A. and the Soviet Union were discharged. The scenario has been popularized in this country by Carl Sagan. It affirms that the explosion of many nuclear weapons would liberate an immense cloud of dust and smoke into the atmosphere and that this would encircle the earth. The rays of the sun would find it difficult to penetrate this cloud and the result would be a substantial drop in temperature. This would lead to an expansion of the icefields and the reduction or elimination of the growing season for food. The result would be a massive world famine in which the majority of the world's population would die of starvation.

Some claim that such a nuclear winter would not come to pass. Nevertheless, the possibility that it might come to pass is adequate to restrain all but the suicidal from launching or extending a nuclear war. The restraint would be particularly effective in the Soviet Union where the problem of growing sufficient food is chronic.

2. *U.S. Self-destruction:*

The communist rulers are guided by the doctrines of Marxism-Leninism. These doctrines teach that capitalism is terminally ill and patience is indicated while America self-destructs.

The communists see many signs that capitalism is in its death throes. These signs are both economic and social. In the economic realm, they point to unemployment, the plight of the homeless, the international banking crises, and the intractible deficit. In the social realms they point to the increase in vice and crime, corruption in high places, educational deterioration, racial discrimination, the alienation of youth, terrorism, and the AIDS epidemic.

Their doctrine also teaches them that progress is inherent in history, so communist world victory is inevitable. However, progress proceeds by a series of advances and retreats, just as a hammer drives a nail. Therefore, retreat is as essential as advance in their strategy. If a nuclear war seems imminent, retreat is indicated. To them retreat is not defeat.

3. *Success of Their Current Strategy:*

The success of their current worldwide programs confirms their conviction that they are on the path to the establishment of the "World Dictatorship of the Proletariat" and that nuclear war is both unnecessary and undesirable. These programs operate under the umbrella of peaceful coexistence. . . .

The Role of Nuclear Weapons

If there is to be no nuclear war, what is the role of nuclear weapons? Are they useless and irrelevant? By no means. They have a most important function to perform in the communist campaign for conquest.

This function can be illustrated by reference to American football. A football team has two elements—the ball carriers and the blockers. The function of the nuclear weapons can be likened to that of the blockers.

The primary role of the blockers is to protect the ball carriers, especially the quarter-back, so that they may advance the ball towards their opponent's goal line.

In the great conflict between the forces of communism and those of the free world, the ball carriers are the National Liberation Revolutions such as those taking place in El Salvador, the Philippines, and South Africa; the national communist parties; the subversive fronts; communist espionage; and communist propaganda. These advance the cause of communism towards victory.

The communists regard any "National Liberation Revolution" as a step towards a "Socialist" revolution. When a national liberation revolution removes a country from the ranks of the free world, the communist ball is advanced several yards.

The existence of nuclear weapons in communist hands prevents the forces of the U.S.A. from taking effective action to prevent such developments. The possibility of causing nuclear war paralyzes the American will. When the Hungarian freedom fighters cried out for help, none was given because it might start a nuclear war. The same situa-

Illustration by Craig MacIntosh

Reprinted with permission of the *Minneapolis Star and Tribune.*

tion prevailed when the forces of freedom in Czechoslovakia were attacked by the armed might of the Soviet Union and its Warsaw Pact allies. An identical situation today limits U.S. assistance to Solidarity in Poland and the Afghan people. Many in Congress are opposing giving help to Jonas Savimbi and the forces of UNITA in Angola despite the presence of 30,000 Cuban troops along with Soviet and East German forces fighting for the ruling Marxist-Leninist tyranny. They fear escalating hostilities that might lead to nuclear war. Nuclear weapons are most effective blockers.

Conclusion

The communists are most reluctant to become involved in nuclear war. The part to be played by their nuclear weapons is made clear by the formula which they are following as they plot, work, and fight to conquer the U.S.A. This formula is:

"External encirclement, plus internal demoralization, plus thermonuclear blackmail, lead to progressive surrender."

The assurance that our future is not threatened by a nuclear war should not be a sedative inducing apathy and slumber. It must be an alarm bell warning us of the advances the forces of communism are making towards their victory.

To extend the football analogy, we need ball carriers as well as blockers. We must not put our trust in military weapons alone, but we must have a game plan that employs skilled, talented and dedicated truth bearers who will propel the ball of liberty over the goal line of security for all mankind.

The selection, training and support of such ball carriers can be given without the slightest risk of causing nuclear war.

PREVENTING A NUCLEAR HOLOCAUST

WE ARE CLOSE TO EXTINCTION

Union of Concerned Scientists

The Union of Concerned Scientists is a non-profit organization dedicated to ending the nuclear arms race and greatly reducing nuclear arsenals.

Points to Consider

1. Why are we entering a new stage of instability in the nuclear arms race?
2. What is the doctrine of limited war?
3. Why have arms control negotiations failed?
4. What actions must be taken to prevent nuclear war?

Excerpted from a position paper by the Union of Concerned Scientists in 1983.

We are driven toward war by the spread of nuclear weapons to many nations and even, in coming years, to terrorist groups.

Each day, three to five new nuclear warheads are constructed on this small planet.

And with every day that passes, we are driven closer to the possibility that the terrible destructive force of nuclear weapons will be unleashed.

The United States and the Soviet Union must bear the chief responsibility for this awful danger. They are engaged in an escalating nuclear contest in which each strives for an illusory military superiority over the other—a superiority which cannot be achieved because neither side can or will allow it.

We are entering a new age of instability. We are moving into a time in which nuclear war is becoming increasingly probable—unless we act now, unless we act together.

But first, we must fully understand the forces which are propelling us toward war.

The Doctrine of Limited War

We are propelled toward war by the evolution of a military doctrine that the "limited" use of nuclear weapons can counter set-backs in conventional military battles and "win" the resulting conflict.

It assumes that the use of nuclear weapons, once begun, could be constrained and would not escalate into a nuclear war of global magnitude. "Limited war" proponents ignore, at our ultimate risk, the warnings of leading military authorities who believe that a nuclear exchange could not be terminated until it had escalated into a global catastrophe.

We are driven toward war by the spread of nuclear weapons to many nations and even, in coming years, to terrorist groups. Some of these nations have a history of instability or violent confrontations with others. These simmering antagonisms could lead to the use of nuclear weapons and escalate into the nuclear involvement of the superpowers.

116

The Failure of Arms Control Negotiations

We are propelled toward war by the failure of both sides to seriously negotiate mutual nuclear arms limitations. For the past decade, we have seen arms talks sometimes used by both the superpowers as propaganda vehicles rather than as forums for good faith bargaining.

Time and again, we have seen unrealistic proposals put forth which seem plausible to a public unaware of the intricacies of weapons technology and the complexity of the strategic balance, but which are known in advance to be unacceptable to the other side. New weapon systems have been advanced as "bargaining chips", but all too often they have become integral parts of the nuclear arsenal, never to be traded away. . . .

Preventing Nuclear War

The Union of Concerned Scientists believes that nuclear war can be prevented if enough people will join together in a movement with rational goals based on a step-by-step approach toward mutual reductions in our ability to destroy each other.

As Americans, citizens of the United States, we have a special responsibility in this effort. The rapidly expanding American and Soviet nuclear arsenals are the most threatening in the world, especially since leaders of both nations appear to sincerely believe that blustering words, hard-line postures, and more and more nuclear weapons are a better means of achieving security than earnest diplomacy.

To prevent nuclear war, we must be pragmatic. UCS recognizes that present realities require a strong American defense system. We know that the leaders in the Kremlin are not idealistic peacemakers. Events around the world have demonstrated this all too well in recent years.

Therefore, we do not call for unilateral arms reduction.

But we in the United States must recognize that a truly strong defense must not and can not be built around urgent planning for the actual use of nuclear weapons.

We must have a defense based on a different doctrine, a different strategy, so that our defense system will cease to be as great a menace to ourselves as it is to those it is designed to deter.

Impact on Children

The psychological impact on children and adolescents "living in a world where thermonuclear disaster is a constant threat" was the subject of a study conducted between 1978 and 1980 by the American Psychiatric Association. The results, recently published by Harvard psychiatrists Dr. John Mack and Dr. William Beardslee, indicated that among 1000 Boston, Los Angeles and Baltimore grammar and high school students, "the imminent threat of nuclear annihilation has penetrated deeply into their consciousness." A majority admitted that the nuclear threat had discouraged their thoughts about marriage, even their plans for the future. Most said it influenced their daily thinking and feeling. Compared to research studies of twenty years ago, the APA study showed a marked increase in the level of children's nuclear anxiety.

Jane Wales, Physicians for Social Responsibility, May 14, 1986

The UCS Program

First, UCS believes that it is crucial that the U.S. and the Soviets immediately halt the introduction of weapons systems which would destroy the balance upheld over the past three decades—systems, such as the MX missile, the neutron bomb and the Soviet SS-18, which, by their very nature, make a nuclear war more, not less, likely.

So UCS joins in the call for a mutual freeze on the build-up of nuclear weapons as an important step toward elimination of the threat of war. The Freeze is based on a straightforward idea: that the U.S. and the U.S.S.R. should each stop testing, building and deploying these weapons which are capable of destroying our civilization.

A Freeze on nuclear weapons, particularly on strategic warheads and missiles, would be a positive, symbolic first

118

step by the superpowers, signifying to the world and to each other that they are willing to call a halt to the arms race. By itself, however, the Freeze would still leave humanity facing the threat of the 50,000 nuclear weapons now in the super-power arsenals. So we must also look beyond the Freeze.

The adoption of the policy of "No First Use" of nuclear weapons would be an important and effective next step. Most Americans are surprised to learn that it is United States policy to use nuclear weapons *first* in the event NATO is unable to repell a non-nuclear Warsaw Pact attack. UCS is working to expose the risks and weaknesses of this concept and to replace it with a more rational and secure approach.

We advocate a policy of "No First Use" which would greatly reduce American reliance on nuclear weapons to de-fend against conventional attack. Under this policy, nuclear weapons now deployed near sensitive borders could be removed entirely, substantially lessening the risk that a nuclear war would erupt out of a local conflict.

UCS has led in the promotion of the policy of "No First Use." We began by obtaining the endorsement of this con-cept by leading scientists, including 43 Nobel Laureates and over 500 members of the National Academy of Sciences.

This has developed into an important public education program, including publication of our major report entitled "No First Use." We have been pleased to see this policy gain acceptance by the American people, including the sup-port for "No First Use" in the recent pastoral letter of the National Conference of Catholic Bishops.

While such initiatives move forward, UCS will continue to press for our long-term goals such as the implementation of a comprehensive program of detailed negotiations covering all nuclear forces.

We are aiming not only for a nuclear Freeze but also for greatly reduced arsenals by the end of this decade, as well as a negotiated end to the testing of nuclear bombs. And UCS believes that a global program can and must be developed for curtailing the spread of nuclear weapons to other nations.

Public Education

Public education remains our central objective. UCS is ef-fective because our efforts are coordinated in an overall

campaign to educate policymakers, the media, and the general public about the issues of nuclear weapons and arms control. This is particulary important when it comes to our youth, the leaders of tomorrow.

In co-operation with the National Education Association, UCS has developed and promoted Choices, a series of junior high school lessons on nuclear war which is currently being used in school systems across the nation. Choices has come under strong attack by the Reagan Administration, which has designed lessons of its own to promote the idea that children should believe there is no problem with nuclear war.

On the college level, UCS has, since 1981, sponsored and produced special materials for a series of annual programs, the UCS Veteran's Day Convocations. These "teach-ins" on nuclear weapons and arms control are held each year at as many as 500 institutions.

UCS publications play an important public role as well. Beyond the Freeze, our book on the solutions to the arms race, provides an historical perspective on the policies which have brought us closer to nuclear war and suggests that there are effective remedies to ease the threat of nuclear holocaust. No First Use, a study conducted under the direction of Vice Admiral John Marshall Lee (USN, Ret.), assessed NATO's capability to defend itself without nuclear weapons.

In addition, UCS has produced numerous other brochures, reports, and studies, a half-hour film on "No First Use" and has worked closely with the national media to help reporters and editors understand the intricate issues involved in arms control.

PREVENTING A
NUCLEAR HOLOCAUST

CIVIL DEFENSE AND SURVIVAL:
THE POINT

Leon Goure

Dr. Leon Goure is the director of the Center for Soviet Studies for the Science Applications International Corporation.

Points to Consider

1. Why could reducing nuclear weapons stockpiles make nuclear war seem safe?
2. What relationship does nuclear winter have to civil defense?
3. What different kinds of nuclear winter scenarios are possible?
4. How does the Soviet Union view nuclear winter and civil defense?

Excerpted from testimony by Leon Goure before the House Committee on Science and Technology, September 12, 1984.

With adequate food stocks and preparations, a country may be able to feed and sustain its surviving population through a year of adverse climatic conditions while preparing to reconstitute essential agricultural production.

The authors of the "Nuclear Winter" study, R. P. Turco, O. B. Toon, T. P. Ackerman, J. B. Pollack and Carl Sagan (hereafter referred to as TTAPS), offer an apocalyptic prediction of possible global climatic consequences of a large nuclear exchange. This prediction critically depends on the amount of soot particles injected into the troposphere by numerous large urban fires which may result from nuclear strikes. Under certain circumstances, the effects on climatic conditions generated by the fire-produced soot may be significantly aggravated and protracted by the amount of fine dust particles lofted into the stratosphere by surface and near-surface detonations of nuclear weapons.

At the present time, as the authors of the TTAPS study acknowledge, there are many uncertainties about the phenomenology underlying the key parameters believed to be essential to produce a "Nuclear Winter." For purposes of this discussion, however, it is assumed that the "Nuclear Winter" hypothesis represents an accurate prediction of what may occur in certain nuclear war conditions. Even so, it is important to note that the "Nuclear Winter" effect is very much scenario dependent. . . .

Arms Reductions

In the context of the "Nuclear Winter" hypothesis, the question is what particular significance it has for such arms reduction. In his Foreign Affairs article (Winter 1983-1984), Dr. Carl Sagan urged a drastic reduction of the existing stockpiles to below what he called the "Doomsday Threshold," that is, below the level where the use of the weapons could trigger what he characterizes as "the climatic catastrophe." . . .

While the concept of avoiding a "climatic catastrophe" by reducing strategic nuclear weapons stockpiles to some level

Millions of Fatalities

"Under the worst conceivable circumstances, a profligate exchange targeted at populations and without any civil defense preparations on either side would result in 219 to 265 million fatalities among the populations of the combatant nations.
Office of Technology Assessment, 1979

below the "Nuclear Winter" threshold appears attractive, it may have the effect of making the waging of nuclear war seem "safer" to contemplate. It may be argued that rather than reducing the stockpiles below such a threshold, effective deterrence of nuclear war may be enhanced by the possession by both the United States and the Soviet Union of capabilities to threaten each other with "Nuclear Winter." After all, for years many people have equated strategic stability and effective deterrence with the capability of both superpowers to threaten each other with mutual assured destruction. It could be argued, therefore, that the mutual threat to cause a "Nuclear Winter" may be equally or even more stabilizing and deterring. Furthermore, such a capability may enhance prospects for restraint in the use of nuclear weapons in the event of a war and for intra-war escalation control and negotiations. Thus, at least for the present, the "Nuclear Winter" hypothesis does not provide an obvious answer to the question concerning the level to which strategic nuclear weapons stockpiles could be safely reduced.

War Survival Measures

At the present stage of its development, the "Nuclear Winter" hypothesis does not negate the utility of passive defense measures and preparations aimed at mitigating the consequences of the prompt effects of nuclear detonations as well as of "Nuclear Winter." There are various reasons for this.

First, as was noted, unless significant elements of the nation's population are protected against and survive the

124

prompt effects of nuclear detonations and radio-active fallout, and possibly also chemical and bacteriological attacks, the predicted subsequent "Nuclear Winter" effect may be largely academic from the standpoint of national survival.

Second, any "Nuclear Winter" effect would be certain to cause more damage to the country which is unprepared to mitigate its consequences for the population and the economy, than to the country which has made such preparations. An asymmetry between belligerent countries in civil defense capabilities and preparedness may result in different levels of damage to them and also in different perceptions of the consequences and acceptability of various degrees of severity of "Nuclear Winter."

Third, as the TTAPS study shows, the severity and duration of the "Nuclear Winter" vary and are very much scenario dependent. One need not a priori assume that only the worst case TTAPS scenario is the most likely one. In other scenarios the adverse climatic conditions, if they occur, may be far more survivable, especially if appropriate preparations are made for such contingencies. Furthermore, if the "Nuclear Winter" is a realistic threat, it is not unreasonable to assume that the belligerents would be likely to exercise restraint in their use of force and in the choices of targets; this in turn would increase the effectiveness of civil defense and other disaster mitigating measures.

Fourth, in the matter of the ecological consequences projected in the "Nuclear Winter" hypothesis, the TTAPS scenarios assume the start of the nuclear exchange to take

place in June. In other words, they assume a worst-case situation in which the ecology in the northern and mid-latitudes of the Northern Hemisphere would suffer maximum damage from a sharp decline in air temperatures and reduction in the amount of sunlight reaching the Earth's surface. However, presumably a less damaging situation to the belligerents would occur if the strategic exchange were to take place when the plants in those latitudes are dormant, ie., in winter. In the TTAPS baseline scenario, return to near ambient sunlight and above freezing air temperatures in the interior contaminated areas are projected to be reached in some 100 days or less. If fewer cities burn than is assumed in the scenario, a return to near ambient sunlight conditions would occur even sooner, and if there is less dust in the stratosphere, the duration of lower temperatures would be shorter. In other words, the worst conditions would not last much longer than the winter. Indeed, given that in the first year after an exchange prospects for agricultural production in the belligerent countries will be poor for reasons of disruption of the economy, if not because of some sort of "Nuclear Winter" effect, it would be logical for an aggressor to initiate his attack only after he has harvested his crops and not before as the TTAPS scenarios assume. An attack in that season of the year would have also the advantage that probable meteorological conditions in the belligerent countries, ie., snow, rain, fog, overcast, etc., would tend to mitigate the secondary effects of nuclear detonations such as fires and also increase the rate of rainout of soot and dust in the troposphere. With adequate food stocks and preparations, a country may be able to feed and sustain its surviving population through a year of adverse climatic conditions while preparing to reconstitute essential agricultural production. In his Foreign Affairs article Dr. Sagan acknowledges that this may be a possibility, although he mentions that the "breakdown of civil order and transportation systems" may prevent effective support of the population. Such a "breakdown," however, is by no means inevitable, although whether or not it occurs will depend in a large measure on the effectiveness of pre-attack civil defense planning and preparations. Certainly the Soviet civil defense program expects to ensure both civil order and an organized system of support of the population in the post-

attack period. Mention is also made of other possible adverse effects on the ecology such as global radioactive fallout, depletion of the ozone layer, and so forth; however, these are largely independent of the "Nuclear Winter" hypothesis.

Soviet Policies

Given the many current uncertainties about "Nuclear Winter" and its potential strategic implications, it would be premature for any strategic planner, be he American or Soviet, to be guided by this hypothesis. Indeed, the Soviet approach to this question is illustrative. Soviet propaganda, as reflected by political and science spokesmen, has enthusiastically embraced the TTAPS "Nuclear Winter" hypothesis as well as other Western "worst case" nuclear war scenarios in order, as is publicly acknowledged, to influence Western public opinion and U.S. defense programs. The official Soviet public support for the TTAPS hypothesis, however, has had no visible effect on Soviet defense policies. Thus, in recent times, Soviet scientists have been instructed by the leadership to work even harder on the further strengthening of Soviet military might; Soviet military chiefs predict a further build-up of Soviet offensive strategic nuclear weapons; and the utility of Soviet civil defense and the need to further perfect it continues to be extolled.

Of course, if additional studies and analyses confirm the "Nuclear Winter" hypothesis as constituting a realistic possibility, it is possible that eventually this may significantly influence strategic planning and weapons programs, as well as arms control negotiations. However, to use this hypothesis for such purposes at this time, as some are attempting to do, would seem to be unwarranted.

PREVENTING A NUCLEAR
HOLOCAUST

CIVIL DEFENSE AND SURVIVAL: THE COUNTERPOINT

Leon Baya

Leon Baya wrote the following article for the Daily World, *the official publication for the Communist Party USA. The article was a review of the book* Last Aid: The Medical Dimensions of Nuclear War, *edited by Eric Chivian, M.D. and others.*

Points to Consider

1. Why can there be no shelter from a nuclear war?
2. What would be the medical effects of a nuclear war?
3. Who was General T.K. Jones and what did he say?
4. What should be done to prevent nuclear war?

Leon Baya, "Nuclear Survival Myths," *Daily World,* August 17, 1983, p. 9.

This book, the result of a meeting of International Physicians for the Prevention of Nuclear War, proves quite conclusively that there can be no shelter, nor even any survival from such a catastrophe.

The Reagan Administration has allocated close to a quarter of a billion dollars to erect a shelter system in case a nuclear war breaks out. It has, in addition, earmarked another $2 billion in the next three years to expand this plan. Yet, this book, the result of a meeting of International Physicians for the Prevention of Nuclear War, proves quite conclusively that there can be no shelter, nor even any survival from such a castatrophe. The authorities who met to discuss the issue of possible survival or receiving medical aid, and who arrived at this dismal conclusion include: Jonas Salk, discoverer of the Salk vaccine that wiped out the crippling polio virus, and who is now the head of the highly regarded Salk Institute, which does intensive virological research at La Jolla, California; Academician Nikolai N. Blokhin, President of the Soviet Academy of Medicine; John Boag, United Kingdom Emeritus Professor of Physics as Applied to Medicine, University of London; Dr. Naomi Shohno of the Hiroshima Jogakuin College and Chairperson of the Study of Nuclear Problems, and 73 other distinguished physicians and psychiatrists in the field from more than 25 countries, both socialist and capitalist. These distinguished people met in Airlie, Virginia to discuss the issue.

Potential Nuclear War

The book begins with an account, and provides some gruesome photos, of the atom bombing of Hiroshima and of Nagasaki. We see burned corpses piled high; we see mutilated faces, distracted people seeking family, relatives and friends; we see children and older people lying hopelessly in beds waiting for death to take them, mercifully, from their pain and intense suffering. Yet this horrible bombing will be insignificant compared to the potential of a nuclear war which will be wrought with weapons hundreds and hundreds of times more powerful than the "baby bombs" dropped so callously on the civilian population of Japan.

130

Two Billion Victims

A report released Tuesday by the World Health Organization estimates that about half the world's population of 4.5 billion would be "immediate victims" of an all-out nuclear war.

The report, prepared by an international committee of 10 scientists, listed a potential toll of 1.15 billion dead and 1.1 billion injured in outlining the worst of three war scenarios that it said "do not include the extreme views."

It warned that the chances of injured survivors receiving any medical attention are "next to nil" and voiced doubt that "even a comprehensive civil defense policy would reduce significantly the number of casualties."

Associated Press, May 11, 1983

Medical Aid

The unavoidable conclusion of these world-recognized discussants is that there cannot possibly be any aid for any of the victims of a nuclear war. Neither medical men, nor hospitals, nor nurses, nor medicine will be made available, for entire cities will lie in ruins. Community life will be totally destroyed. How will those who 'survive' get medical aid amid the confusion and destruction? How will the poisoned water, air and soil be done away with when radioactivity has a half life of some 56,000 years, and then retains its poisons for a decreasing amount for another equal period of time? What assurance is there that hospitals and medical men and women will, themselves, remain alive? How can whatever medicines that are available be reached? Given these indisputable facts, arrived at by this impartial committee of noted authorities, how logical can this statement be, made by General T.C. Jones, Deputy Under Secretary of Defense for Strategic and Theater Nuclear Forces:

"In case of a nuclear war, dig a hole, cover it with a couple of doors and then throw three feet of dirt on top. It's the dirt that does it. If there are enough shovels around, everybody's going to make it!"

Manke, Deutsche Volkszeitung

General Jones doesn't even believe in the necessity, futile as it is, of shelters! (Read Robert Scheer's **With Enough Shovels** for further elaboration of this absolute absurdity.)

Ironically, the book quotes President Reagan who, on April 14, 1982 at Camp David, said, "A nuclear war cannot be won and must never be fought." Yet his latest "Star Wars" scenario would put nuclear weapons into space.

Conclusions

The book's conclusions have been endorsed by George F. Kennan, former ambassador to the Soviet Union, and Admiral Noel Gayler, U.S. Navy, Retired, who says, **"LAST AID** demonstrates in compelling and factual detail the overwhelming consequences and military futility of nuclear war. After reading this, no sane leader can contemplate the use of nuclear weapons for any purpose whatever, military or political." Nuclear war is also condemned by Admiral Hyman Rickover, the "father" of our nuclear submarines, who now has come to realize the horror of a nuclear war.

The book concludes with an appeal from the committee to both the Soviet Union and the United States to refrain from resorting to nuclear war.

This fine book can be of great service in proving the absolute necessity for all of us to prevent the outbreak of a nuclear war that could spell doom for humankind and this very unique planet.

WHAT IS POLITICAL BIAS?

This activity may be used as an individualized study guide for students in libraries and resource centers or as a discussion catalyst in small group and classroom discussions.

Many readers are unaware that written material usually expresses an opinion or bias. The skill to read with insight and understanding requires the ability to detect different kinds of bias. Political bias, race bias, sex bias, ethnocentric bias and religious bias are five basic kinds of opinions expressed in editorials and literature that attempt to persuade. This activity will focus on political bias defined in the glossary below.

5 Kinds of Editorial Opinion or Bias

*sex bias— *the expression of dislike for and/or feeling of superiority over the opposite sex or a particular sexual minority*

*race bias— *the expression of dislike for and/or feeling of superiority over a racial group*

*ethnocentric bias— *the expression of a belief that one's own group, race, religion, culture or nation is superior. Ethnocentric persons judge others by their own standards and values.*

*political bias— *the expression of political opinions and attitudes about domestic or foreign affairs*

*religious bias— *the expression of a religious belief or attitude*

Guidelines

Read through the following statements and decide which ones represent political opinion or bias. Evaluate each statement by using the method indicated below.

Mark (P)   for statements that reflect any political opinion or bias.

Mark (F)   for any factual statements.

Mark (O)   for statements of opinion that reflect other kinds of opinion or bias.

Mark (N)   for any statements that you are not sure about.

_____ 1. The strategic defense initiative promises to end the threat of nuclear winter as well as the fear of nuclear war.

_____ 2. "Everybody's going to make it if there are enough shovels to go around. . . . Dig a hole, cover it with a couple of doors and then throw three feet of dirt on top. It's the dirt that does it."

_____ 3. "A consensus of more than 100 scientists at a conference on *The World After Nuclear War* revealed that a large-scale nuclear exchange could mean the extinction of the human race."

_____ 4. The Soviets and the Americans together have over 50,000 nuclear weapons.

_____ 5. There are vastly too many nuclear weapons in the world.

_____ 6. Either superpower could unilaterally reduce its number of nuclear weapons by many thousands of weapons without harming the security position of its nation.

_____ 7. The superpowers have always prohibited nuclear war by means of deterrence, so the notion of nuclear winter will not change their strategic nuclear policies.

_____ 8. The theory of nuclear deterrence means that a nation could respond to any nuclear attack by destroying the nation that launched the first strike.

_____ 9. Reviews and studies by scientists in all fields have confirmed the theory of nuclear winter.

_____ 10. Nuclear war is God's will and there is nothing man can do to stop it.

_____ 11. We need not be too concerned about the physical world since it is the spiritual world that is most important.

____ 12. A first nuclear strike is no longer feasible since nuclear winter would eventually destroy any nation launching a first nuclear strike.

____ 13. What we need first is a mutually verifiable nuclear freeze.

____ 14. The Soviets are clearly ahead of the U.S. in the nuclear weapons race.

____ 15. The uncertainties surrounding the theory of nuclear winter are too numerous for anyone to take the theory seriously.

____ 16. Because of nuclear winter, the chance of any nation risking the use of nuclear weapons is greatly reduced.

____ 17. There will probably be a nuclear winter in my life-time.

____ 18. Even if nuclear winter renders humans extinct, intelligent life will evolve again.

____ 19. A strong civil defense program could save our nation from the ravages of nuclear winter.

____ 20. The only defense against nuclear war is through political understanding and not through technological superiority.

Other Activities

1. Locate three examples of *political opinion* or *bias* in the readings from chapter four.
2. Make up one statement that would be an example of each of the following: *sex bias, race bias, ethnocentric bias,* and *religious bias.*

Bibliography

Center for Aerospace Doctrine, Research, and Education, 1984: **Nuclear Winter and National Security: Implications for Future Policy.** Air University Press, Maxwell Air Force Base, AL.

Cess, R.D., 1985: **The Climatic Effects of Large Injections of Atmospheric Smoke and Dust: A Study of Climate Feedback Mechanisms With One- And Three-Dimensional Climate Models,** Journal of Geophysical Research.

Committee on Science and Technology, U.S. House of Representatives, 1983: **The Consequences of Nuclear War on the Global Environment,** U.S. Government Printing Office, Washington, D.C.

Covey, C., Schneider, S.H. and Thompson, S.L., 1984: **Global Atmospheric Effects of Massive Smoke Injections from a Nuclear War: Results from General Circulation Model Simulations,** Nature.

Covey, C., Thompson, S.L. and Schneider, S.H., 1985: **Nuclear Winter: A Diagnosis of Atmospheric General Circulation Model Simulations,** Journal of Geophysical Research.

Crutzen, P.J. and Birks, J.W., 1982: **The Atmosphere After a Nuclear War: Twilight at Noon,** AMBIO.

Crutzen, P.J. and Galbally, I.E., 1984: **Atmospheric Effects From Post-Nuclear Fires,** Climatic Change.

Department of Defense, 1985: **The Potential Effects Of Nuclear War On The Climate,** Office of the Secretary of Defense, Washington, D.C.

Ehrlich, P.R., et al., 1983: **Long-Term Biological Consequences of Nuclear War,** Science (This paper was published with Turco et al, 1983—the TTAPS paper—and with it forms the definitive statement of the nuclear winter hypothesis.)

Goure, L. 1984: **Soviet Exploitation of the "Nuclear Winter" Hypothesis,** Science Applications International Corporation, VA.

Goure, L. 1984: **Some Potential Strategic Implications of the "Nuclear Winter" Hypothesis,** Science Applications International Corporation, VA.

MacCracken, M.C., 1983: **Nuclear War: Preliminary Estimates of the Climatic Effects of a Nuclear Exchange,** Paper presented at Third International Conference on Nuclear War, Erice, Sicily, August 19-23, 1983.

MacCracken, M.C., 1985: **The Atmospheric Effects of Post Nuclear Fires: Findings and Uncertainties,** Paper presented to Nuclear Winter Symposium, National Academy of Sciences, March 26, 1985.

MacCracken, M.C. and Walton, J.J., 1984: **The Effects of Interactive Transport and Scavenging of Smoke on the Calculated Temperature Change Resulting From Large Amounts of Smoke,** Paper prepared in the proceedings of the International Seminary on Nuclear War 4th Session: The Nuclear Winter and the New Defense Systems: Problems and Perspectives, Erice, Italy, August 19-24, 1984.

Malone, R.C., Auer, L.H., Glatzmaier, G.A., Wood, M.C. and Toon, O.B., 1985: **Nuclear Winter: Three-Dimensional Simulations including Interactive Transport, Scavenging and Solar Heating of Smoke,** Journal of Geo-physical Research.

National Academy of Sciences, 1975: **Long-Term Worldwide Effects of Multiple Nuclear-Weapons Detonations,** NAS Press, Washington, D.C.

National Academy of Sciences, 1985: **The Effects on the Atmosphere of a Major Nuclear Exchange,** NAS Press, Washington, D.C.

National Climate Program Office: NOAA, 1985: **Interagency Research Report For Assessing Climatic Effects of Nuclear War.**

Office of Technology Assessment, 1979: **The Effects of Nuclear War,** U.S. Government Printing Office, Washington, D.C.

Palomar Corporation, 1985: **Policy Implications of the "Nuclear Winter" Thesis.**

Pittock, A.B., 1984: **Report on the Status of Studies of the Atmospheric Effects of Nuclear War With Special Reference To Effects on the Southern Hemisphere,** Cooperative Institute for Research in Environmental Sciences, Australia.

Postol, T.A., 1984: **Possible Military and Strategic Implications of Nuclear Winter,** Testimony before the House Science and Technology Committee, Subcommittee on Natural Resources, Agriculture Research, and Environment.

Postol, T.A., 1985: **Strategic Confusion - With or Without Nuclear Winter,** Bulletin of Atomic Scientists.

Royal Society of Canada, 1985: **Nuclear Winter and Associated Effects: A Canadian Appraisal of the Environmental Impact of Nuclear War,** Canada.

Sagan, C., 1983/84: **Nuclear War and Climatic Catastrophe: Some Policy Implications,** Foreign Affairs.

Schneider, S.H., 1985: **Nuclear Winter—Its Discovery and Implications,** 1985 Britannica Book of the Year.

Scientific Committee on Problems of The Environment (SCOPE), 1985: **Environmental Consequences of Nuclear War, SCOPE 28.**

Teller, E., 1983: **Dangerous Myths About Nuclear Arms,** Readers Digest.

Teller, E., 1984: **Widespread After-effects of Nuclear War,** Nature.

Thompson, S.L., Aleksandrov, V.V., Stenchikov, G.L., Schneider, S.H., Covey, C. and Chervin, R.M., 1984: **Global Climatic Consequences of Nuclear War: Simulations with Three-Dimensional Models,** AMBIO.

Thompson, S.L., 1985: **Global Interactive Transport Simulations of Nuclear War Smoke,** Nature.

Turco, R.P., Toon, O.B., Ackerman, T., Pollack, J.B.. and Sagan, C. 1983: **Long-Term Atmospheric and Climatic Consequences of a Nuclear Exchange.**

Turco, R.P., Toon, O.B., Ackerman, T., Pollack, J.B. and Sagan, C., 1983: **Nuclear Winter: Global Consequences of Multiple Nuclear Explosions,** Science. (The so-called "TTAPS" paper, an acronym of the authors' names.)

Turco, R.P., Toon, O.B., Ackerman, T., Pollack, J.B. and Sagan, C., 1984: **The Climatic Effects of Nuclear War,** Scientific American.

U.S. Arms Control and Disarmament Agency, 1979: **The Effects of Nuclear War,** Washington, D.C.

Zraket, C.A., 1984: **Military Impact of Nuclear War.**

Glossary

Analogue   something that is similar to another, providing a basis for comparison.

Coagulation   a scavenging process that removes smoke particles by combining or aggregating smoke and soot particles to form large particles. See "scavenging" below.

Combustibility   ability to catch fire and burn, inflammability.

Dust   airborne soil and rock particles created by nuclear explosions near the ground. Dust is created by actual blasts, not by fires.

Megaton   one million tons; a 1-megaton bomb is equivalent in energy release to 1 millions tons of TNT.

Mesoscale   intermediate modeling scale (10-100 kilometers) used to define the area between local and global scales.

Modeling   using computer hardware and software to perform mathematical calculations which simulate atmospheric conditions and responses.

Optical Properties   refers to the degree to which smoke particles absorb sunlight.

Ozone Layer   a gaseous layer formed in the stratosphere which acts as a shield against penetration of ultraviolet light from the sun.

Plume   an elongated, usually open and mobile column or band of smoke shooting upwards from an intense fire.

Scavenging   the removal of gases or particles from the atmosphere.

Smoke   all airborne particles resulting from combustion.

Soot   the carbon-containing (i.e., black) component of smoke.

Stratosphere   upper portion of the atmosphere normally between 6 and 15 miles above the earth's surface.

Toxic Substances   any of various poisonous substances produced by fires; potentially harmful or fatal to humans and other organisms.

Wash-Out   a scavenging process which removes smoke and soot particles from the atmosphere by water condensation; used interchangeably with rain-out.

Yield   the amount of energy expended by a nuclear explosion, usually expressed in kilotons or megatons of TNT.

Abbreviations

C³I	Command, Control, Communications, and Intelligence
DNA	Defense Nuclear Agency
DOD	Department of Defense
DOE	Department of Energy
FEMA	Federal Emergency Management Agency
GAO	General Accounting Office
IRP	Interagency Research Program
NASA	National Aeronautics and Space Administration
NCAR	National Center for Atmospheric Research
NCPO	National Climate Program Office
NOAA	National Oceanic and Atmospheric Administration
NPT	Non-Proliferation Treaty
NSC	National Security Council
NSF	National Science Foundation
OMB	Office of Management and Budget
OSTP	Office of Science and Technology Policy